CATECHETICAL LEADERSHIP

What It Should Look Like, How It Should Work, and Whom It Should Serve

ADRIÁN ALBERTO HERRERA

THE EFFECTIVE CATECHETICAL LEADER

Series Editor Joe Paprocki, DMin

LOYOLAPRESS.
A JESUIT MINISTRY
Chicago

LOYOLA PRESS.
A JESUIT MINISTRY

3441 N. Ashland Avenue
Chicago, Illinois 60657
(800) 621-1008
www.loyolapress.com

Unless otherwise indicated, all Scripture quotations are from the *New Revised Standard Version Bible, Catholic Anglicized Edition*, copyright © 1999, 1995, 1989. Division of Christian Education of the National Council of Churches of Christ in the United States of America.

Scripture quotations marked NIV are taken from the *Holy Bible, New international Version*™. *NIV*™. Copyright © 1973, 1978, 1984 by International Bible Society. Used by permission of Zondervan Publishing House. All rights reserved.

Cover art credit: iStock.com/GoodGnom.

ISBN: 978-0-8294-4526-8
Library of Congress Control Number: 2017953327

Printed in the United States of America.
17 18 19 20 21 22 23 24 25 26 27 Versa 10 9 8 7 6 5 4 3 2 1

Contents

Welcome to The Effective Catechetical Leader Series

The Effective Catechetical Leader series provides skills, strategies, and approaches to ensure success for leaders of parish faith-formation programs. It will benefit anyone working with catechists, including Directors of Religious Education, pastors, diocesan directors, and catechetical training programs. Combining theory and practice, this series will

- provide practical instruction and printable resources;
- define the role of the catechetical leader and offer specific and practical strategies for leading, collaborating, and delegating;
- offer approaches for leading and catechizing in a more evangelizing way; and
- describe best practices for recruiting, training, and forming catechists; developing a vision for faith formation; forming an advisory board; planning and calendaring; networking with colleagues; selecting quality catechetical resources; handling the administrative aspects of the ministry; and identifying various groups to be catechized and approaches that meet the unique needs of those various groups.

Whether you are starting out as a catechetical leader or have been serving as one for many years, **The Effective Catechetical Leader** series will help you use every aspect of this ministry to proclaim the gospel and invite people to discipleship.

About This Book

The ministry of catechesis is critical to the mission of the Church, and the most critical factor in an effective parish catechetical program is the catechetical leader. But, for these leaders to succeed in their role, they must develop specific leadership skills and competencies. This second volume of *The Effective Catechetical Leader* series closely examines what catechetical leadership should look like, how it should work, and whom it should serve. A few of the key topics covered in this book include how to be a servant leader while still exercising legitimate authority; how to properly and pastorally handle difficult situations and conflict to build community; and how to avoid burnout by delegating responsibility and engaging in collaborative ministry.

1

Put Away the Pedestal:
What Leadership in Ministry
Looks Like

Welcome to Leadership

As you peruse a bookstore or browse books online, you will find no shortage of titles on leadership. The books you find, however, will tend to be confined to three areas: business, sports, and politics. If you are looking to run a corporation, coach a championship team, or rule the world, you'll be in luck! Unfortunately, those books don't translate well to the world of catechetical leadership to which you have been called. While you can learn some general leadership principles from the books typically available on leadership, the truth is that catechetical leadership—pastoral leadership in general—is a very different "animal." Running your catechetical program in the manner of a CEO, a football coach, or a politician simply won't cut it. So, to whom do you look for your example of how to lead? I think you know the answer!

Called to Lead

I still remember those Holy Thursdays I used to witness in the parish where I grew up. I remember people arriving early to prepare to participate in the washing of the feet. Every year, there were different people who participated in this service, people of all ages and from different socioeconomic backgrounds. Nevertheless, what I remember most clearly is the manner in which the middle-aged priest would kneel and, with love, tenderness, and delicacy, touch and kiss the bare feet of people after he poured water on them and washed them. This simple act of service that was given to us by Jesus Christ at the Last Supper struck me as a child and as a young man. A simple, humble priest was called to do his job, which is to serve the people of God. You may be thinking, *But I'm not a priest; my ministry is catechetical leadership!* Trust me: you do not need to be a priest to respond as a pastoral minister with love and tenderness, just as this priest did and continues to do today.

So how do you do this?

You may think that good pastoral ministers came down from heaven, lived in a monastery for a long period of time, were raised in a perfect family, or earned numerous academic degrees in order to serve as they do. The truth is that these things can help but are not required! To be a good pastoral minister, you need only recognize and embrace that you have been called in the most sacred way by God to serve him and his people through the Church in the manner Jesus Christ came to serve. God has given you just the right talents and skills to be used for good; all that's needed is for you to discern how best to use them. (This process will be covered in chapter 4.) While you may have met pastoral ministers who behave as "controllers of the faith," as Pope Francis has occasionally suggested, the Holy Spirit is guiding you to lead with humility. In fact, during his homily at the Mass for the inauguration of his pontificate, Pope Francis encouraged us all to "never forget that authentic power is service." He said this because he knows that as human beings, we are tempted by power. What kind of power, you may ask? The kind that dominates, controls, and manipulates others.

However, as Pope Francis reminds us, in pastoral ministry one is called to serve others and not to be served.

Whether you are a new or an experienced catechetical leader, you know that everyone in your parish has needs. You may feel at times that serving or working for the Church can be overwhelming, because life in general is messy. It comes with deadlines to meet, retreats to plan, projects to attend to, meetings that take your time, trainings, long hours, and so on. Yet, you have responded to God's call because more than likely you felt compelled. Now you are pausing to ask yourself, how can I use my gifts to serve best? In the things I have been called to do, where will I find the strength to lead others to follow Jesus?

Welcome to Servant Leadership

There are different styles of leadership, and each person's style of leadership is unique as well. But in a general sense, we must ask, "What is a leader?" In his book *Servant Leadership Models for Your Parish*, Dan Ebener writes that leadership "is defined . . . as an influence process through which a leader inspires or motivates followers toward a common goal or a shared vision" (12). There are leaders in business, education, government, civic communities—and in our parish communities. We have leaders who use their knowledge and skills to undertake and exercise leadership in a way that enables them to achieve the goals of the group. Nevertheless, there have been leaders in history who have abused their position. Certain leaders have used their influence to exercise dominion—to increase their individual power or to control the masses.

So, what kind of leaders does the Church need, especially in the catechetical ministry? For Catholics, servant leadership is rooted in the gospel and modeled by Jesus Christ as he taught his apostles how to serve. This kind of leadership is eucharistic, because we are called to help people deepen their communion with Christ and with one another. In fact, every Sunday, Catholics are called to celebrate the Christian mystery—otherwise known as Holy Eucharist—because it is an action of thanksgiving to God. Out of gratitude, Catholics all over the world give thanks to God for all the blessings received. I once heard a homily in which the pastor mentioned that Jesus' style of leadership emerged from the strong identity and bond he had with his Father. This unique and intimate connection with the Father helped the apostles to see the constant compassion Jesus had for people. While Jesus' ministry was full of mercy and healing, as described in the Gospels, he also empowered his apostles and people around him to follow a similar path—and isn't that our job as catechetical leaders?

The role of the pastoral minister is to direct people to Christ, to show Christ to others, and, in doing so, to light a fire in people's hearts. Unfortunately, we are sometimes paralyzed by the fear of taking risks and of making changes—both of which are part and parcel of the role of leader. Consequently, we need to be aware of our calling, recognize our abilities, and embrace our limitations when exercising pastoral leadership.

My Introduction to Servant Leadership

Years ago, when I was hired by the Archdiocese of Galveston-Houston as a staff member for the Office of Continuing Education (as it was then called), all my coworkers were older than I and had an impressive wealth of knowledge in catechesis and pastoral care. After I had been on the job a few months, my immediate supervisor approached me about a project the archdiocese was undertaking involving Catholic schools and youth ministry. At that moment, I thought the project would be only a small task and not a massive endeavor. I listened to my supervisor as she explained the vision for the project and she asked if I could create and spearhead a steering committee.

As she left my office, I felt like the prophet Jeremiah: "Alas, Sovereign LORD, . . . I do not know how to speak. I am too young" (Jer. 1:6, NIV). I told her that I needed to think about her proposal and that I would get back to her. I have to admit that there was fear in me—a sense of uncertainty and a feeling of not knowing where to start. I wanted to tell my supervisor I was not the person she was looking for, but I chose not to because I didn't want her to see my fears. I remember driving home that evening feeling like a big weight had been dropped on my shoulders. My head was spinning questions and commentary such as *Why me? I'm just a rookie! She could have asked others.* At the same time, however, there was a part of me that kept whispering, *Take the risk.*

I realized I was facing a spiritual dilemma and decided to see my spiritual director. I shared all my fears and doubts with him, but they started to crumble and fade away when he said, "Take the opportunity. Take the risk." It felt as if God had given me the answer.

I must confess that not every situation works out this way. The project lasted almost seven years, and it involved numerous people from different educational backgrounds. To make a long story short, this experience led to the creation of a new vision for lifelong catechesis for the archdiocese. Days before my supervisor retired, I felt a measure of confidence and asked her why she had chosen me for this project. She replied, "You are young, and I knew that you would be able to do it." She had the ability to recognize gifts and talents that others probably didn't know they had.

I do not tell this story to boast, since the project was an immense collaboration of talented people who made such a vision possible. I tell this story to demonstrate that when a leader shows high levels of confidence and genuine interest in certain followers, the leader establishes trust and builds a sense of commitment that can motivate others to do new and fruitful work. As catechetical leaders, we are called to do the same—to take risks and learn from those risks even when uncertainty prevails and the direction is not clear. Leadership does not come by special revelation but begins, as author Robert Greenleaf suggests, "with the natural feeling that one wants to serve, to serve *first*" (*The Servant as Leader*, 6). Because of this, most team members know intuitively who the real leaders are. The impulse to lead by serving is what is referred to as "servant leadership."

What Is Servant Leadership?

The practice of our faith cannot be separated from our daily lives. What we believe in needs to permeate how we live, how we interact with one another, how we dialogue, and how we work. To become a leader implies that one has followers: the leader has proven trustworthy and is able to guide others into areas or opportunities for growth. In this way of leading, other people's needs—rather than the leader's own—are being served first. This leadership style is therefore known as "servant leadership."

Servant leadership models the leadership style of Jesus. In his book *Servant Leadership Models for Your Parish*, Dan Ebener writes that, like Jesus, servant leaders "serve their followers instead of the other way around. Instead of focusing on their own personal needs and interests, servant leaders are tuned into the needs and interests of both their followers *and* their organizations" (21).

Jesus Christ himself offered his apostles a unique way of leading while serving others. As I have said, the model of leadership the apostles learned from Jesus emerged from his unique and intimate connection with the Father. Jesus' style of servant leadership is evident throughout the Gospels and is characterized by compassion, healing, and forgiveness. In the story of the washing of the feet (John 13:1–17), we are told that Jesus got up from the table, took off his outer garment, tied a towel around his waist, and began to wash his disciples' feet.

After doing this, he asked them if they knew what he was doing and then instructed them to do the same for others. Jesus transformed his apostles by turning them into leaders in a way that was free and not forced. This model of servant leadership brings about the conversion of hearts through love.

Each of the following Bible passages shows how Jesus served others by putting his own interests aside. Take a minute to read each one, and then jot down any words or phrases that describe the kind of servant leadership modeled in that passage.

Matt. 14:13–21	
John 9:1–7	
John 13:1–15	
Matt. 20:20–28	
Luke 10:30–37	
Matt. 25:31–46	
Mark 6:30–33	
John 15:12–17	
Luke 4:38–39	
Luke 7:1–10	
Luke 7:44–50	

What Leadership in Ministry Looks Like

A few years ago, on a visit I made to one of the parishes in our diocese, I met two pastoral ministers who were friends and had successful professional careers. They had been invited by their pastor to oversee adult faith formation in each of their parishes, both of which he was assigned to. The friends were eager to help both parishes and to join forces to create a new model of collaboration for merged parishes. I recommended that they first create a ministry plan to determine how the coordination of this new ministry would be exercised between their two parishes. I also gave them other resources to review and explore. As I left the meeting, I told one of them to persevere and not feel bogged down if parishioners didn't immediately respond to their invitation. "Adrián," he responded, "I owe this to the Lord. It's my way of giving back to him for the countless blessings I have received."

Two months later, the other pastoral minister called to tell me that there had been too much of a struggle for control and that the two friends could not agree which of them would lead, so she had decided to leave the merged parish. This happened because their models of leadership were very different. One minister had a style I call "imposition leadership": his ideas, thoughts, and actions were, to his mind, the only way of carrying out the ministry. He engaged in consultation only when he needed others to carry out a plan. The other minister had a style I call "what-if" leadership: she feared taking risks, was hesitant to take action when needed, and could not get past wondering, "What if we could do it this way?" or "What if we get these people here?" Her ambivalent behavior led to little action.

The inability of the two ministers to merge their leadership styles greatly affected their respective parishes. Parishioners saw a power struggle rather than any real leadership. Two years later, I had a chance to see the imposition leader at an event. Ironically, the first words out of his mouth were, "Adrián, it is so difficult to work for the Church. Everyone wants to be in control!" The truth is, those who are least confident often overcompensate by trying to control people, processes, and situations.

Are we called to a controlling ministry? No, we are not. Unfortunately, however, the Church is seen by many as an institution that should be run like a corporation. Pope Francis, on the other hand, said that the Church needs to be a mother, "not a well-organized NGO [non-governmental organization] with a bunch of pastoral plans."[1]

Leadership is too often understood as a position of power over others. We often believe that because someone is in a particular position, he or she has more control or dominion over people or has the ability to make changes single-handedly. But this need not be the case. Leadership in pastoral ministry should reflect the core values that Jesus taught in the Gospels. Pastoral ministry calls for people who are compassionate, are willing to walk with broken people, and want to serve first as a loving parent does for his or her children. Pastoral ministry, especially in catechesis, calls for leaders who, through character, integrity, and strength, lead people as Jesus himself did with the apostles—a style of leadership rooted in a deep personal relationship with God, who calls, forms, and sends us forth. Servant leaders recognize the sacredness of each person, reaffirm the image of God in that person, and are willing to put the needs of others before their own.

Okay . . . but isn't that the way everyone in a parish should behave? It's regrettable that our brokenness due to sin becomes quite evident when we interact with others, and we forget how to serve as Jesus did. This too often leads to an abuse of power and authority, which undermines the true calling we have received from Jesus Christ to "love one another as I have loved you" (John 15:12). True service begins with the gospel notion of being willing to serve rather than to be served. This disposition surges from a heart willing to create equal ground for all members and inspires others to do the same. In his book *Servant Leadership*, Robert Greenleaf suggests that if someone is placed in a hierarchical authority, they consider themselves not on pedestals looking over people, but instead as *primus inter pares*, or "first among equals." This brand of authority inspires allegiance because it

---

1. http://en.radiovaticana.va/news/2014/06/17/
   pope_francis_church_a_mother_not_a_ngo/1101850.

communicates a unique willingness to serve, which in turn inspires trust. Servant leaders have proven and demonstrated that they are in a position of leadership not through dominion over others but because they are willing to serve and care for others. "The great leader is seen as a servant first," Greenleaf writes (21).

Finally, the *National Certification Standards for Lay Ecclesial Ministers* echoes the theme of servant leadership when it reminds us that catechetical leaders are called to "demonstrate such virtues as honesty and responsibility, generosity and compassion, humility, patience, a passion for justice, and a spirit of service" (#1.1,f).

Summary: The Greatest Must Serve

[Jesus said,] "Whoever wishes to become great among you must be your servant." (Mark 10:43)

Servant leadership is very different from the style of leadership prevalent in the secular world, which tends to be self-serving, individualistic, and cynical. Too often, the emphasis is on achievement rather than on establishing relationships. Servant leadership, by contrast, is about putting the needs of others before one's own and being willing to serve and meet those needs. In turn, the people served feel empowered, grow in their faith, and are willing to join the leader in serving and giving life to the parish.

Effective servant leadership begins with the integrity of the leader. To begin shaping your servant-leadership ministry, ask yourself these questions: *Am I ready to roll up my sleeves and help do whatever needs to be done? If the answer is yes, are my actions consistent with my values and beliefs? In other words, do I walk the walk and talk the talk? Or do my actions lack credibility and integrity? Am I ready to work side by side with others and involve them in decision making? Am I ready to serve the interests and needs of those around me—or simply lead without serving others? Am I ready to lead like Jesus?*

For Reflection and Discussion

- Name a few behavioral characteristics of the people who inspired you to be a pastoral minister.
- Do you have the skills necessary to lead like Jesus? Explain.

Growing as a Catechetical Leader

Leading the people of God requires a willingness to serve others as Jesus did his apostles. Many people want to deepen their relationship with God but lack the confidence or feel unworthy to serve in parish ministry. How do you as a catechetical leader invite others to respond to their baptismal call?

Go to www.loyolapress.com/ECL to access the worksheet.

Suggested Action

Creating a culture of servant leadership among ministries requires putting the needs of others before your own. Consider various ministries in your parish (besides the catechetical one). What needs do those ministries have? What actions can you take to be a bridge builder?

For Further Consideration

Servant Leadership: A Journey into the Nature of Legitimate Power and Greatness. Robert K. Greenleaf (Mahwah, NJ: Paulist Press, 1997).

Servant Leadership Models for Your Parish. Dan R. Ebener (Mahwah, NJ: Paulist Press, 2010).

Principled Ministry: A Guidebook for Catholic Church Leaders. Loughlan Sofield, ST, and Carroll Juliano, SHCJ (Notre Dame, IN: Ave Maria Press, 2011).

National Certification Standards for Lay Ecclesial Ministers. (Alliance for the Certification of Lay Ecclesial Ministers, 2011).

2

Where Are You Taking Us?
Leadership and Articulating
a Vision

Doing the Right Things

I mentioned earlier that, while they may not be the perfect models of leadership for us to consider in pastoral ministry, the worlds of business, sports, and politics offer some insights into the nature of leadership. For example, they help us know, right off the bat, that there is a difference between *management* and *leadership*. According to Warren G. Bennis and Burt Nanus in their book *Leaders: Strategies for Taking Charge* (New York: HarperCollins, 2003), "Managers are people who do things right and leaders are people who do the right thing" (20). While you most certainly want to learn to do things right, it is important to remember that you have been called to catechetical *leadership*, not catechetical *management*. In his book *The 7 Habits of Highly Effective People*, the late Stephen Covey explained that management is concerned with efficiently climbing the ladder of success, while leadership is concerned with ensuring that the ladder is "leaning against the right wall" (101). He goes on to describe managers as those people trying to cut through the jungle with machetes, while a leader is the one who climbs up a tall tree to shout, "Wrong jungle!" (101). In your role as a catechetical leader, you are called to climb the tallest tree to survey the landscape and determine the best direction to move in. You are called to place the "ladder of success" against the right wall. You are called not just to do things right but to help ensure that your parish faith-formation program is doing the right things. In other words, you are called to have vision.

Vision: The Ability to See

Jesus' penchant for healing people with blindness did not stem from a fascination with optometry. Rather, he was concerned with vision—the ability to see not only physically but also spiritually. As a catechetical leader, you are called to articulate a vision for those you serve. Whereas a mission statement describes the reason an organization exists (including priorities, responsibilities, and actions), a vision statement describes, in inspirational language, what a desired change or outcome of a particular action will be; it "paints a picture" of what the mission will look like when it comes to fruition as a result of specific actions and initiatives. Throughout the history of the Catholic Church, numerous people have articulated a vision of what it means to follow Christ. In fact, the people we call saints are canonized precisely because their lives provide a vision for living as a disciple of Jesus. Among those saints who accomplished this noble task are the martyrs—those whose vision of the kingdom was so powerful that it compelled them to offer their very lives for its sake.

Why Are We Called to Serve?

The 2016 movie *Silence*, directed by Martin Scorsese, depicts two seventeenth-century Jesuit priests traveling to Japan from Portugal to locate their missing mentor, Fr. Ferreira, who is rumored to have committed apostasy at a time when Christianity in Japan is forbidden and seen as contrary to the traditional way of life. In one village, the two Jesuits encounter and minister to Christians who worship in secret and are persecuted by a samurai known as "the inquisitor." Villagers who refuse to abandon their Christian faith are strapped to wooden crosses and placed in the shallow waters of the ocean to be drowned by the incoming tide. One of the priests, Fr. Rodrigues, goes through a series of emotional ups and downs as he watches people die for believing in Christ and, finally, is captured by the soldiers of the inquisitor and imprisoned. Later, he is invited by the inquisitor to reject the Christian faith in public or face torture, to which Fr. Rodrigues replies, "The blood of martyrs is the seed of the church"—a line attributed to the early Christian writer Tertullian, circa AD 197.

It was through the witness of the martyrs that the early church came to understand what it means to lose one's life in order to gain eternal life. As a catechetical leader, although you may face opposition from time to time, you will most likely (and thankfully) not experience dramatic persecution for the sake of your beliefs—but you have nevertheless been called to lead people and to give witness to your Christian faith by "laying down your life" for others. This is the reason we are called to serve: to help others gain eternal life through the teachings of our Lord Jesus Christ.

What Is the Urgent Need?

Some time ago I was conducting a workshop on *Evangelii Gaudium* for directors and coordinators of adult faith formation, and I had spent the entire morning explaining the first two chapters of this apostolic exhortation. A good number of parishes from across the archdiocese were represented at the workshop, from small parishes with a DRE who does it all to megaparishes with larger staffs and much more robust budgets. During the lunch break, two gentlemen from very well-established parishes asked this question: "Adrián, Pope Francis keeps talking about a conversion of the heart in our attitudes and ministries, and we have been doing this for more than eighteen years. Why the urgency now, when people still come and are being served—plus, our pastor doesn't really care as long as money is collected?" I was stunned by the question because I thought I had made very clear points as to where the church was moving. Nevertheless, I told them that this was more than a reason to re-evangelize, given the large numbers of people leaving the Catholic Church overall, especially among Hispanics who have left to join Pentecostal or charismatic movements not in communion with the Catholic Church.

The need was very obvious, not just within their ministries but also in their own attitudes and biases. This is where real conversion is truly needed in pastoral ministry—where we think we have it all figured out and have fallen into the temptation of letting our initial love for the Lord grow cold. Catechetical leadership needs to be invigorated so that we allow the Holy Spirit to take action and shake us out of our complacencies. For this to happen, an internal examination of conscience is always needed. As I was driving home after the workshop, I kept thinking, *When will the church become proactive rather than reactive when it comes to evangelization?* So much is at stake that I have made the following exclamations of Saint Paul my own: "Woe to me if I do not proclaim the gospel" (1 Cor. 9:16) and "Now is the acceptable time" (2 Cor. 6:2).

As leaders in catechetical ministry, we cannot continue to minister only for the sake of meeting our budgets and timelines, maintaining our ministries, or reacting to the signs of the times. Instead, we must recognize the urgency of the need for the kind of evangelization or re-evangelization that leads to the personal conversion of all involved. Pastoral ministry today more than ever is challenged by society to go out for the sake of the gospel of love. Credible Christian witness is urgently needed, not only in our parishes but also in the public sphere. These ideas should not be left out when drafting a vision for your ministry, because a significant part of articulating a vision for ministry is creating a sense of urgency. In *A Church on the Move,* Joe Paprocki refers to John P. Kotter's book, *Leading Change,* in which he explains that transformation is difficult in groups where complacency runs high and that complacency takes over when people don't recognize a visible crisis, have low expectations and narrow goals, are out of touch with those they are supposed to serve, and hear only "happy talk" from their leaders. Without a sense of urgency, he writes, we can easily allow our attention to be diverted to trivial things.

Urgency does not mean that we need to act quickly but that we need to draw attention to things that deserve our immediate and undivided attention. In her book *The Preaching Life*, Barbara Brown Taylor warns that without a sense of urgency, we tend to "lose our voices, to forget where we were going and why" (5). She warns that unless we bring our best efforts to our ministry, the church could someday be relegated to an exhibit in a museum.

So What *Is* the Mission of the Church?

Both vision and mission are required for real change. We all know the biblical passage from the Gospel of Matthew, "Go thereforeand make disciples of all nations, baptizing them in the name of the Father and of the Son and of the Holy Spirit, and teaching them to obey everything that I have commanded you" (Matt. 28:19–20). This is the mission for every leader in the catechetical world. Moreover, the *Catechism of the Catholic Church* is very explicit as to what kind of road the Church is called to walk:

"This mission continues and, in the course of history, unfolds the mission of Christ, who was sent to evangelize the poor; so the Church, urged on by the Spirit of Christ, must walk the road Christ himself walked, a way of poverty and obedience, of service and self-sacrifice even to death, a death from which he emerged victorious by his resurrection (*CCC*, #852)." So it is that "the blood of martyrs is the seed of Christians."

Likewise, Pope Paul VI, in his apostolic exhortation *Evangelii Nuntiandi*, teaches that "evangelizing is in fact the grace and vocation proper to the Church. . . . She exists in order to evangelize, that is to say . . . to be the channel of the gift of grace, to reconcile sinners with God, and to perpetuate Christ's sacrifice in the Mass" (#14). Along the same lines, Pope Francis calls for a renewal within the Church that would lead away from the status quo and toward true transformation and evangelization:

> I dream of a "missionary option" . . . capable of transforming everything, so that the Church's customs, ways of doing things, times and schedules, language and structures can be suitably channeled for the evangelization of today's world rather than for her self-preservation. (*Evangelii Gaudium*, #27)

The Church is very clear on its mission, which is to "walk the road Christ himself walked." As a catechetical leader, you must be clear about which road you are called to venture upon to serve and lead people to Christ, and to do so as Jesus did.

Dreaming for a Vision

In *Dreams and Visions: Pastoral Planning for Lifelong Faith Formation*, Bill Huebsch explains that at the very minimum, a plan needs to be put in place so that you can move from "being a very good parish to being one that is really *great*" (126). For instance, let's say that you have a great adult faith-formation program at your parish, but you want to make it even more vibrant. Your pastor tells you that there are other ministries needed in the parish, such as a sponsor-couple ministry, marriage-preparation teams, and so on, and asks if you can make that happen. You don't have to start from scratch since you already have a good adult faith-formation program; instead you can use this opportunity as a channel of grace to develop other ministries. As you begin to dream about the vision, you will see that you will be able to cover three essential areas with this approach.

1. You will meet the needs of your parishioners.
2. You will help them grow in their faith and relationship with Christ.
3. Their sense of belonging and confidence will increase.

Then you will be ready to make invitations for others to join you in the specific ministries needed. To empower people in this way, you must first take some essential steps to create a clear vision for your ministry. The following steps are adapted from Huebsch's *Dreams and Visions* (132):

Steps in the Visioning Process

1. Commit to the vision and process and get the right people to help. (The pastor and staff members need to endorse the process.)
2. Study the history of your parish, including its strengths and weaknesses.
3. Do a needs assessment of your ministry, as well as of the parish.
4. Hold an informational meeting with top personnel, and mark this as the first step in the process.
5. Invite the parish at large to participate in visioning.
6. Form the right team. You need both visionaries and people who understand the need.

   a. Identify and create a hospitality group to make arrangements for physical details of gatherings.
   b. Identify and create a prayer-and-process group to organize content, schedules, and procedures for gatherings.

    c. Identify and create a data-collection group to compile basic facts to be presented at gatherings.

    d. Identify and create a resources group to curate resources in key areas.

    e. Identify and create a communication/publicity group to organize the promotion and publicity of events.

7. Talk with specific groups you hope to reach within the parish.
8. Form leaders.
9. Prepare a short vision statement.
10. Share back with the parish at large.
11. Begin the implementation process.

Visioning does not need to be done by one person alone. Thankfully, we have national organizations such as NCCL (National Conference for Catechetical Leadership) that can inspire, motivate, transform, create, and drive the vision of professional catechesis in our parishes. As this vision of professional ministry in catechesis is formed, it allows the creation of a culture of faith formation that is consistent across the nation. The document *Co-Workers in the Vineyard of the Lord*, published by the United States Conference of Catholic Bishops (USCCB), explains that professional ministry requires the ongoing formation that can occur through "diocesan, regional, or national conferences, and active participation in the work of diocesan, regional, and national ministerial associations" (51)—so please, avail yourself of these communities and resources!

How to Create and Articulate a Vision

Every day, you awaken with a vision of the day ahead. You "picture" what you are going to eat for breakfast, what you are going to wear, and how you are going to get your day started. A vision is basically that: a picture of the future. As a catechetical leader, you are called to articulate a vision for faith formation in your parish community. This vision will guide all future decisions, provide motivation, and create much-needed cohesion among all parties involved. Everything that happens can be measured by the extent to which it lines up with the articulated vision.

A good way to begin the process of creating a vision for your faith-formation program—in addition to asking the Holy Spirit for guidance and inspiration—is to imagine someone three or four years down the line writing a positive review of your parish faith-formation program for a local newspaper. What would he say are its most positive, attractive, and effective features? What would she say is most unique? What would they offer as the single most important reason why people in the area should want to participate in your parish's faith-formation program?

As you draft your vision statement, keep in mind that the best vision statements are

- imaginative but also practical; they are both sensible and achievable.
- desirable and inspiring; they propose a preferred future.
- clearly focused; their desired outcomes are observable.
- flexible; they leave room for the Holy Spirit.
- easily communicated; they can be articulated in a thirty-second "elevator speech."

Until you can put a check mark next to each of these criteria, your vision statement isn't finished.

To guide my thinking during this process, I used questions like the following. You can use versions of them as you create a vision statement for your catechetical ministry.

- What will be different in our parish in three to five years because our catechetical ministry exists?

- What role(s) will our catechetical ministry play in making the difference?
- Who will be our catechetical ministry's partners or collaborators in this effort?
- What will our catechetical ministry be known for in three to five years?
- What do our parishioners think about our catechetical ministry today?

Once you've finalized your vision statement, it's time to articulate it, or share it with the parish community. In essence, articulating a vision requires the following four things:

1. **Proposing an appealing and inspiring picture of the future**—for example: "Within five years, the faith-formation program of _____ parish will be a model for empowering parents to embrace their role as the primary educators of their children."

2. **Offering a method for implementing the vision**—for example: "This will be achieved by introducing an alternate model for faith formation—family catechesis—that will gradually replace the traditional model for children's faith formation."

3. **Identifying specific steps and a timetable for implementation**—for example: "In year one, we will educate the faith community about the role of parents as primary educators of their children; in year two, we will introduce an alternate family catechesis model to run alongside the traditional model; in years three and four, we will grow and strengthen the family catechesis model so that it becomes seen as the primary model for faith formation; in year five, we will discontinue the traditional model for children's faith formation and continue to grow and strengthen the family catechesis model."

4. **Implementing an action plan that is in line with the vision**—executing the above steps with adjustments as required.

As mentioned above, a crucial aspect of articulating a vision statement is actually articulating—communicating—it to people. A vision should be referred to constantly, consistently, and in simple language. It always helps to propose and use a metaphor or symbol that captures and illustrates the vision. (For example, Pope Francis articulates his vision of the church as a "field hospital.") Most important, you yourself need to embody and exemplify the vision in your thoughts, words, and actions. Your "way of proceeding" should be consistent with the articulated vision.

My Own Experience of Creating a Vision

I have personally used this process of visioning in my own parish pastoral council. Several years ago, I was nominated to be a member of the council and then was elected chair. During the first meeting I attended, it was evident the council had many struggles related to organizational and attitudinal issues, as well as a lack of vision about what a parish pastoral council could do. I soon realized that there were two challenges that needed immediate attention. I called them 1) internal structure and organization and 2) external image of the council.

Internally, council members had different understandings of what a council was charged to do. As a result, there were many voices leading in many different directions—and you can probably imagine the pastor pulling his hair out! Externally, most parishioners thought a parish pastoral council should behave like a city council, one that hears and resolves issues legislatively. None of these understandings was accurate.

The first thing I did as chair was to explain the issues to the pastor and other staff. Second, I consulted with the proper offices of the archdiocese to see what resources were available to address these challenges. Third, I expressed the need for a vision statement for the council and initiated work on this among council members. Fourth, I arranged for consultation with other members and ministries of the parish. Fifth, all feedback was brought back to the council and then reported to the parish at large. Finally, we drafted a vision statement, as well as objectives and a pastoral plan for the parish.

A Passion for Carrying the Vision

Author Robert Greenleaf distinguishes between the vision and passion that drive your efforts and the energy and emotions required to carry out the vision. As catechetical leaders, we need all in order to evangelize and transform the world in which we live.

How do we maintain our passion to make disciples of Christ when our models or strategies may not be as effective as they were ten years ago? In his book *Reimagining Faith Formation for the 21st Century*, John Roberto suggests that Christian faith needs to be more holistic by involving the head, the heart, and the hands. Roberto suggests that there are three essential components all leaders should consider when forming a new vision.

1. relational community
2. intentional practice
3. experiential belief

Let's look at each of these components in turn.

Relational Community

Forming a relational community means going the extra mile to get to know people rather than just be acquainted with them. It means making followers the way Jesus did with his apostles. In the Gospel of John, when two of John the Baptist's disciples asked Jesus where he was staying, he replied, "'Come and see' . . . and they remained with him that day" (John 1:39). Andrew later told his brother Simon Peter that they had found the Messiah. We don't know exactly what kind of conversation took place, but we can speculate that it was a positive, engaging, and transforming experience. Jesus invited his first two disciples to be with him; servant leadership calls for creating a similarly relational community that allows for complete abandonment to God and, as the *National Directory for Catechesis* states, "loving assent to all that he has revealed" (#99).

When he was the archbishop of Buenos Aires, Pope Francis (then Cardinal Jorge Bergoglio) experienced such a relational community by visiting the "villas of Buenos Aires," or poor shantytowns and slums with little or no sanitation and with a proliferation of drugs, violence, and dire poverty. During his pastoral visits, the people of the "villas" truly felt the archbishop of Buenos Aires was their bishop because he lived their struggles, their joys, and their griefs. This is what we call *acompañamiento* or, as *Evangelii Gaudium* calls it, the art of accompaniment, "which teaches us to remove our sandals before the sacred ground of the other" (#169). Elisabetta Piqué writes in her book about the life of Pope Francis that Bergoglio devoted his attention and affection to the people of the villas because "he believes that the shantytowns hide a treasure that can do good for the whole church—the deep faith and simple piety of the people" (*Pope Francis: Life and Revolution*, 145). Relational community is directly linked to the way servant leadership is shaped: through a willingness to serve and meet the needs of others.

Intentional Practice

The second aspect John Roberto describes is intentionality, an acute sense of self-awareness or self-consciousness. Intentional evangelizing efforts are consciously conceived, planned, and organized. Such intentionality requires practice, practice, and more practice. The good news is that the more you do it, the more it becomes an extraordinary and powerful discipline.

As catechetical leaders, we are called to provide opportunities for people to grow in their faith and to nurture a strong commitment to building bridges, healing wounds, and respecting others. We are asked to lead as Jesus did. Think about how you recruit catechists—disciples—for your ministry. Do you issue an open invitation from the pulpit to the parish? Is recruiting catechists a quest to fill holes with warm bodies? Or do you take time to be selective and discern who possesses the charism for such ministry? Investing the time in the latter approach will pay off in the long run. A deliberate and intentional recruiting practice will result in a paradigm shift that enables people to recognize their own call to live out their baptism in service to others.

And isn't that what Jesus did with his disciples? He took the time to visit with them. He got to know them. He spent time with them and then issued the invitation to follow him. We can commit ourselves to an intentional practice like Jesus' if we are fully aware of the dire need to motivate others and fully willing to take risks to make disciples for the Lord. In doing so, we will improve not only our effectiveness as catechetical leaders but our strategy for evangelizing as well.

Experiential Belief

Experiential belief refers to celebrating life through rituals, milestones, and liturgical seasons. As catechetical leaders committed to making disciples, we must provide spiritual and liturgical formation opportunities by participating in the customs and rituals of our Catholic tradition. Young children as well as adults are more fully engaged when all their five senses are involved in experiences of prayer or liturgical ritual. Anyone who experiences affect is more likely to value church and make a personal connection with Jesus. As Pope Francis observes in *Evangelii Gaudium*, "the Church is not a tollhouse; it is the house of the Father" (#47).

Summary: Visioning for the Future

"Lord, to whom can we go? You have the words of eternal life."
(John 6:68)

Catechetical ministry is much more than a program, and it isn't just about learning the basic tenets of the faith or sacramentalizing children. Rather, catechetical leaders, along with parish staff, are called to dream, create, and shape a broad vision for the ministry. This vision should include all the people of a parish and aim to motivate them to follow Christ and give witness to the Catholic faith. Most important, it should lead the people of your parish into a communal life of discipleship.

For Reflection and Discussion

- What motivates you to carry out your pastoral service? What is your vision for catechesis?
- In your view, what human attitude or qualities should the pastoral minister have in order to arouse enthusiasm in and thus share faith with others?

Growing as a Catechetical Leader

Your role as a catechetical leader is to help people see the big picture of catechetical ministry by making disciples as Jesus did. This includes building bridges, healing wounds, and strengthening relationships.

Go to www.loyolapress.com/ECL to access the worksheet.

Suggested Action

The key to a successful visioning process is to remember that you are not alone. Begin by sharing your thoughts and ideas with your pastor and pastoral staff, and make a habit of communicating your dreams and visions for catechetical ministry to key individuals.

For Further Consideration

Evangelii Nuntiandi: On Evangelization in the Modern World. Pope Paul VI (Boston: Pauline Media, 1976).

Evangelii Gaudium: Apostolic Exhortation on the Proclamation of the Gospel in Today's World. Pope Francis (Washington, DC: United States Conference of Catholic Bishops, 2013).

Reimagining Faith Formation for the 21st Century. John Roberto (Naugatuck, CT: Lifelong Faith Associates, 2015).

Co-Workers in the Vineyard of the Lord: A Resource for Guiding the Development of Lay Ecclesial Ministry. (Washington, DC: United States Conference of Catholic Bishops, 2005).

Leading Change. John P. Cotter (Boston: Harvard Business Review, 2012).

3

Avoiding the Superhero Approach: Leadership, Collaboration, and Delegation

Busyness in Ministry

Not long ago, my wife and I were preparing for the celebration of our daughter Fatima's first Eucharist. We talked about all the small details—details that, admittedly, I would have overlooked on my own. The conversation covered topics such as the quality and color of the tablecloths, the decorations, the music, the cake, the dress, and the guest list. That night we ended up creating a checklist. Each of us was assigned specific duties and responsibilities. As the weeks went by, we would occasionally check in with each other to see if there was anything missing or if help was needed. When the day of the celebration came, I was a proud papa as I watched my daughter receive her first Eucharist.

Before the celebration, my head was spinning, running through the mental checklist to see if I had forgotten something along the way. We had everything that we needed for the reception. Invitations had gone out, the perfect cake had been ordered, tablecloths had been secured and music planned for. The celebration began, and it was beautiful to see all the little angels with their shining faces ready to receive the body and blood of Christ. My eyes fixed on the face of my daughter, and I began to contemplate her. I could not stop thinking about how much she had grown in such a short time. Then I felt a surge of guilt go through my body for losing so much time along the way. Had I been as present to her as I could have been throughout her first eight years of life? Sure, I was home in the evenings, awakened her every morning, took her to school, took her to her pediatrician for shots when needed, accompanied her to soccer practice, and so on. Nevertheless, my heart was longing for those precious moments I may have missed.

Later that night, once everything was over, I felt kind of gloomy. My wife noticed. She asked me if there was anything wrong with the party. No, I replied, everything had gone splendidly. I then shared with her how I was feeling. I told her that God was giving me a second chance and that I was going to use my time more diligently and not allow myself to sacrifice family time because of professional ministerial responsibilities.

Don't get me wrong! I love my ministry and enjoy sharing my faith with others, but as catechetical leaders, we can easily get caught up in the overwhelming details of our ministry and forget to focus on the opportunities right before us. In my case, I had been too busy paying attention to the tasks of raising children and had forgotten an essential aspect of fatherhood—enjoying my children!

The Lone Ranger and Silo Mentalities

Although catechetical ministry is a specific role in the Church and has an influence on other ministries, it is often too easy for us as catechetical leaders to be tempted to carry out the ministry by ourselves. Too often, we feel that, to build competence, we have to be productive and get in the business of competition for the sake of power. We feel that if things are not done directly by us, people may think that we are incapable of serving and leading others. As a result, we end up adopting a

"Lone Ranger" mentality—the belief that we should try to do it all by ourselves.

I remember growing up watching the movie *Rambo* because my dad was a fan of Sylvester Stallone. You may recall that in the movie, Sly portrays a former Green Beret and Vietnam War veteran known as John Rambo, who travels by foot to visit one of his old comrades and learns, upon his arrival, that his friend has died from cancer. Rambo continues to travel and, on his way to a town in Washington, is spotted by Sheriff Will Teasle, who considers him to be suspicious. When Rambo asks Teasle for directions to a diner, the sheriff offers to take him but instead drives him out of town and tells him not to return. Rambo does return, after which he gets arrested on charges of vagrancy and resisting arrest. Teasle's officers bully and abuse Rambo, which causes flashbacks to the torture he endured during the war in Vietnam. As a result, he unleashes his rage. Rambo escapes and flees into the woods, where he survives by using his combat skills to disable all the deputies who are out looking for him. Rambo is the typical Hollywood hero: someone who can achieve victory completely on his own.

Why do I tell this story? Sometimes as catechetical leaders we tend to act like Rambo. We think that we can do it all by ourselves while isolating the gifts and talents of others in the parish. When we try to survive on our own, we end up on the defensive, just like Rambo. We also end up disabling the very people we should be enabling!

Closely related to the "Lone Ranger" mentality is the "silo" mentality—an approach to ministry that keeps us focused solely on our own area of responsibility to the exclusion of other ministries. Thus, the faith-formation program becomes a world unto itself, while the liturgical program and the social-justice program follow suit.

Pope Francis makes it clear how a community of disciples, which includes the catechetical leader, is called to live:

The Lord gets involved and he involves his own, as he kneels to wash their feet. He tells his disciples: "You will be blessed if you do this" (Jn 13:17). An evangelizing community gets involved by word and deed in people's daily lives; it *bridges* distances, it is willing to abase itself if necessary, and it *embraces* human life, *touching the suffering flesh* of Christ in others. (*EG,* #24, emphasis added)

In a silo culture, people in ministry struggle to engage other people collaboratively. It feels like "pulling teeth." A pastor once told me that he was trying to create a culture of collaboration with several of his own staff by having regular meetings. Even though people were quite prepared to attend the meetings and make a few observations, once the meeting was over, they went back to doing their business as usual and did little to communicate with others until the next meeting. There was no real change. This type of mind-set and systemic dysfunction in the parish could be attributed to human personalities. However, it is in direct opposition to what it means for us to function as a church.

As catechetical leaders who are called to lead as Jesus did, we need to stay away from this type of behavior. Silo mentality only nurtures the ego; it creates barriers instead of bridges, dividing instead of seeking unity; it encourages disconnected decision making; and, most important, it forgets how to be an evangelizing community.

If Only They Had Talked to One Another!

To illustrate my point, I offer the following example that I once encountered. The parish has a director of religious education and a director of adult faith formation. Both leaders are employed by the parish and have specific responsibilities for carrying out the ministry of faith formation. Their offices are in different buildings, and once a month they have staff meetings with the pastor. At one staff meeting, the director of adult faith formation was unable to attend because of an illness. However, the DRE was present and reported that she saw a need for offering a retreat in a few months' time to the parents of children preparing for sacraments. Unfortunately, it never occurred to the DRE to ask the director of adult faith formation whether there was already a retreat in place, instead of reinventing the wheel.

She spent two months trying to put a retreat team in place, got all the legal forms signed and submitted, created the content of the retreat, designed a fancy registration flyer, and bought the things she needed, all while carrying out her operational duties as a DRE. She got completely overwhelmed to the point of exhaustion.

The following month, there was no staff meeting because of the holidays, so the topic did not come up again. Eventually the DRE had her retreat, and 45 out of 110 parents attended. They had a wonderful experience, but in the end, it was too much for the DRE. At the next staff meeting, shortly thereafter, the director of adult faith formation reported that he was promoting a retreat for the following month to all adults of the parish on the topic of personal transformation and family dynamics. He had a team of people helping him promote, lead, and facilitate the retreat, which had more than 180 participants.

Well, you may ask, what happened? Obviously there was no communication between the catechetical leader and the director of adult faith formation, and a low level of collaboration among staff was evident. The pastor or the pastoral associate could have told the DRE that before embarking on creating this retreat, she should first speak to the director of adult faith formation and see how the two of them might join forces. This could have saved time, energy, and resources and allowed the DRE to carry on with greater effectiveness.

Collaboration

The first step in collaboration is to recognize that you are a talented catechetical leader; that's why you were hired to do the job. However, there are other talents and gifts in your parish that can help you carry out your ministry. Collaboration is more than just a nice idea; it is essential for the mission of the church and is an expression of the "oneness" that characterizes the Body of Christ. In a sense, collaboration is the "default setting" for Christians and is not a strategy but a spiritual practice. Collaboration means to work together to meet the needs and interests of multiple parties—not just your own. Your role as catechetical leader is to bring forth the different gifts of all to accomplish the task at hand. This begins with a common vision to be an evangelizing community that brings Christ to all sectors of society.

Moreover, collaboration means that as leaders, we need to learn to let go of our own egos and eliminate the presumption that we have all the gifts and answers people are looking for. In his book *Servant Leadership: A Journey into the Nature of Legitimate Power and Greatness*, author Robert Greenleaf describes ego as "tyrannical, despotic, and dictatorial. . . . [It] sees relationships in terms of threat or no threat" (Paulist Press, 1997, 6). When our egos are not disciplined, they are incapable of serving the needs of others—something that can only be done when we recognize the sacredness and image of God in each person. Collaboration breaks this vicious cycle of trying to control because it sees and values a greater good for the community and not just one's own self-preservation.

The following table (adapted from *Effective Collaboration*, published by Llywodraeth Cymru, [the Welsh government; see http://learning.gov.wales/docs/learningwales/publications/ 150922-info-booklet-en.pdf]) shows the outcomes of effective and ineffective collaboration.

Noneffective Collaboration	Effective Collaboration
Competition	Community
Rule bound	Value and vision driven
High control	High trust and consent
Top-down authority	Shared authority
Coercive approach	Positive influence

Collaboration requires time, freedom, effort, willingness, and active listening—which, according to Robert Greenleaf, "builds strength in other people." Collaboration also avoids internal competition, adversarialism, micromanagement, and controlling relationships. Catechetical leaders can become effective collaborators by being

- active listeners who are willing to engage
- clear communicators
- authentic in their expectations
- leaders who foster structures that allow for collaboration
- willing to lead by example—a credible witness
- adaptive and evolving
- aware of the broad picture or common good
- willing to delegate responsibilities
- willing to empower others

Collaboration could best be summarized as working together by building upon one another's strengths and gifts.

Collaboration from the Beginning

In their article "New Evangelization through Collaboration," Fr. Frank Donio, SAC, and Barbara Humphrey McCrabb identify three distinct types of collaboration: "collaboration for," which is characterized by one person making a decision and then inviting others to implement the plan; "collaboration with," which is characterized by one person inviting a few others to work together with him or her to effect change; and "collaboration from the beginning," which relies on working in a communal fashion throughout the entire process, not as a strategy but as a "way of proceeding" (*Catechetical Leader*, November 2014; see http://www.catholicapostolatecenter.org/uploads/9/2/4/6/9246931/ new_evangelization_through_collaboration_nov.pdf).

This collaborative way of proceeding is characterized, according to Donio and McCrabb, by what they refer to as cenacle spirituality, *communio* ecclesiology, and cooperation technology.

- **Cenacle Spirituality**—The upper room where the disciples and Mary gathered in prayer in anticipation of the coming of the Holy Spirit on Pentecost is traditionally referred to as the "cenacle" (from the Latin word *cenaculum*, for "dining room"). According to Donio and McCrabb, a cenacle spirituality is one that recognizes the gifts of all, united under the guidance and advocacy of the Holy Spirit, who animates the group to gather in prayer and to go forth in mission.

- ***Communio* Ecclesiology**—*Communio* is a unity that goes much deeper than mere fellowship and togetherness. It refers to the inner life of the Trinity, an intimacy so intense that Three Persons are One. Our collaboration is not simply with one another but with the Trinity.

- **Cooperation Technology**—Ultimately, collaboration is manifested through nuts-and-bolts techniques that include recognizing one another's gifts and engaging in reciprocal dialogue, deep listening, and effective responding. Donio and McCrabb explain that this cooperation is characterized by being simple and direct, proactive and outward-focused, pastoral and collaborative, merciful and joyful, and faith-filled and witnessing.

Collaboration, for the catechetical minister, is not simply something that might help improve effectiveness but is rather a call to embody the life of the Trinity—the ultimate model of collaboration.

The Art of Delegation

There are some catechetical leaders who are willing to help, serve, and do the job, but don't ask other people for help or delegate responsibilities because they want to show people that they are capable. There are others who do the job without asking for help because they want to please everyone. In his book *Servant Leadership Models for Your Parish*, Dan Ebener explains that a leader who tries to do everything and does not delegate is practicing "service without power" (20). A leader can end up being trampled by others because he or she lacks the power to influence and make strategic changes according to the need.

Once again I think of my own experience working with the parish pastoral council. I had to delegate responsibilities to the vice-chair and to other members of the council by encouraging them to take initiative. It wasn't just dumping responsibilities onto them because I didn't want to do my job. Rather, I delegated responsibilities because I recognized the different gifts and talents this council possessed. I'm not the council; I'm only a member of the council, and this ministry is not mine but has been provided to me by the authority of the Church. The same principle can be applied to the catechetical ministry. Do you personally call the parent of each child who missed a class? No; the effective catechetical leader might delegate this by, say, forming a group of parents who help make those calls. In such a case, the responsibility of the catechetical leader is to provide the calling team with a list of names, phone numbers, and a script that is pastorally sensitive and not offensive for them to read. After that, the task will get done.

Delegation begins with a personal invitation—which requires actual eye-to-eye human contact. Ebener describes how members of

Saint Mary's Parish in Iowa City got involved by getting a "tap on the shoulder" either by Fr. Ken or by Sr. Agnes, inviting them to help (108). Jesus himself has given us the best possible model for tap-on-the-shoulder invitations; he walked around Galilee, getting to know people—and then the personal invitation came.

Take a moment and look up the following Bible passages describing how Jesus invited others to join him. Jot down any words or phrases that show human contact, warmth, or inclusiveness.

Luke 7:36–50	
Luke 14:8–14	
John 1:35–39	
John 1:43–51	
Matt. 4:18–22	
Matt. 9:9–12	
Mark 10:17–25	

Empowerment

In my role with the Archdiocese of Galveston-Houston Office of Evangelization and Catechesis, I oversee adult faith formation for Spanish-speaking people. Some time ago, after listening to several pastors and people from different ministries, I concluded that the archdiocese needed a retreat that explored different types of spirituality and offered different types of spiritual experiences. I went back to my office and began making calls to retreat centers and to people who might be willing to help me lead this ministry. Later, I visited different parishes and talked to catechetical and Hispanic-ministry leaders in an effort to find people who were willing to serve, willing to listen, and willing to be leaders.

As people were suggested, I observed their ministries and made efforts to get to know them. After several months and a process of discernment, I chose eight people and invited them to form a retreat team named *Qados*, which is related to the Hebrew word *qadosh*, meaning "holy." I provided each team member with a list of responsibilities that included meeting dates and the themes of future retreats. I knew that this was going to require a great deal of effort and time, but the relationship I had established with them was based on trust, and I had great confidence that they could do this.

As a catechetical leader, sharing your ministry with capable partners will help you get the job done. This concept of sharing your ministry is what is meant by empowering others. Sociologists say that strong teams are magnets for talent; forming such teams requires a lot of time and effort, but getting the right people to help you achieve your ministry is well worth it. So, as you begin to collaborate, delegate, and empower others by sharing your ministry, keep in mind that while your team members will help you achieve your goal, the litmus test for true servant leadership is whether those served grow as persons and are more likely themselves to become servants (see Robert K. Greenleaf, *The Servant as Leader*, 6).

Summary: The Beauty of Working with Others

[Jesus said,] "The harvest is plentiful, but the laborers are few; therefore ask the Lord of the harvest to send out laborers into his harvest."
(Luke 10:2)

Servant leaders put the needs of others before their own. And yet it is so easy to fall into the trap of doing things on your own, without asking for help. As catechetical leaders, it is important to acknowledge that catechesis is part of the overarching process of making disciples for the entire parish. At the same time, inviting others to be part of your ministry models the Body of Christ—a community of believers.

Finally, there is beauty in working with others, especially when parish staff are involved. This level of engagement requires effective communication, collaboration, and delegation skills in order to spread the good news of Jesus Christ to others.

For Reflection and Discussion

- What responsibilities do you have that you could delegate to others?
- How do you communicate across various ministries in your parish?
- How do parishioners communicate with you?

Growing as a Catechetical Leader

An important aspect of catechetical ministry is the fact that this ministry is not mine but rather has been provided to me by the authority of the Church to carry out its mission. To do so, collaboration and delegation are needed as more and more people share in this ministry. There can be no Christian "Rambos." How do you invite others to share in your ministry? Is it in your nature to dictate rather than to consult and involve others? If so, what single step can you take to begin the shift toward collaboration?

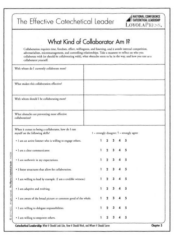

Go to www.loyolapress.com/ECL to access the worksheet.

Suggested Action

Sergey Brin and Larry Page met while in college at Stanford and later founded the company that would become Google. At first they found each other obnoxious, but through their talents and willingness to collaborate, they were able to transform how the world seeks information. Set aside five to ten minutes each day to talk to the staff of your parish, get to know the leaders of different ministries in your parish, and make a list of possible collaborative projects, otherwise known as dreams.

For Further Consideration

Evangelii Gaudium: Apostolic Exhortation on the Proclamation of the Gospel in Today's World. Pope Francis (Washington, DC: United States Conference of Catholic Bishops, 2013).

Hispanic Ministry in Catholic Parishes: A Summary Report of Findings from the National Study of Catholic Parishes with Hispanic Ministry. Hosffman Ospino (Huntington, IN: Our Sunday Visitor, 2015).

Heroic Leadership. Chris Lowney (Chicago: Loyola Press, 2005).

Leadership Is an Art. Max DePree (New York: Penguin Random House, 2004).

Fostering Leadership Skills in Ministry. Jean Marie Hiesberger (Liguori, MO: Liguori Publications, 2002).

4

Got What It Takes? Leadership and Core Competencies

Strengthening Your Core

There is no denying that parishes, movements, dioceses, and national organizations are constantly looking for individuals with the capabilities and skills necessary to carry out catechetical ministries in a professional and effective manner. The *National Directory for Catechesis* states, "The single most critical factor in an effective parish catechetical program is the leadership of a professionally trained parish catechetical leader. . . . Depending on the scope of responsibilities, the position is usually titled 'parish director of catechesis or religious education,' [or] 'parish coordinator of catechesis or religious education'" (#5).

Perhaps you were invited to take on the role of catechetical leader because they needed someone at the parish to enroll students, order textbooks, assign catechists, and run the meetings with the parents. Now that you are in this position, you recognize that the role requires far more than fulfilling a few basic functions. Or perhaps you personally felt a calling to lead people to Jesus through the catechetical ministry, recognizing that the ministry requires a wide range of qualities, skills, and abilities that you are eager to integrate and master. However you arrived and whatever skills you possess, the bottom line is that catechetical leadership is a complex ministry requiring specific core competencies in order to excel.

In the world of physical fitness, a great deal of attention is given to the concept of "strengthening your core." The idea is that if you can strengthen your core muscles, they will stabilize you and enable you to engage in a wide variety of physical activities with greater ease, less pain, and better balance. In a similar way, it is imperative that you as a catechetical leader "strengthen your core"—that is, pay attention to the core competencies that serve as the foundation for all you do in pastoral ministry.

The *National Certification Standards for Lay Ecclesial Ministers*, created by the Alliance for the Certification of Lay Ecclesial Ministers and approved by the United States Conference of Catholic Bishops Commission on Certification and Accreditation, describes four formational categories that are applicable to catechetical leadership—human, spiritual, intellectual, and pastoral—and sets a standard for the core competencies that are directly called for in the document *Co-Workers in the Vineyard of the Lord.*

Human Formation

When you are tended to by a doctor, it helps a great deal if, in addition to medical knowledge, he or she also possesses a good bedside manner. As a catechetical leader, you are dealing not primarily with doctrine and concepts but with people: other human beings. At the heart of your ministry is the ability to build, nurture, and sustain relationships. Those you serve and minister to want to know that you have a healthy and well-balanced personality. This means paying attention to your physical, emotional, sexual, and psychological health and demonstrating the ability to empathize with others, to express and receive warmth and affection, to celebrate joy, and to be reflective. A person who has core competency in human formation displays maturity, character, and a well-balanced personality. He or she manifests "psychological health marked by integrity, appropriate interpersonal boundaries," and the ability to honor and safeguard the trust that people place in his or her as a minister.

In simple terms, a healthy human formation is shown in a catechetical leader who exhibits self-understanding and self-awareness, physical, emotional (including sexual), and psychological health, the ability to grow and learn, an appreciateion of diversity, and basic virtues, especially respect for others.

In order to develop these elements of human formation, *Co-Workers in the Vineyard of the Lord* also recommends that the pastoral minister engage in small faith communities, invite affirmation and critique, participate in counseling and/or spiritual direction, and engage in spiritual reflection (37).

Spiritual Formation

I once knew a pastor who was what people refer to as a "bricks and mortar" kind of guy. He devoted most of his attention and energy to fixing roofs, paving parking lots, renovating parish centers, and coordinating capital campaigns. Yes, these are all very important and worthwhile endeavors. But this pastor also seemed incapable of sharing his faith or expressing any deep spiritual thought, which led people to wonder why, exactly, he ever became a priest.

Spiritual formation is very closely linked to human formation but focuses on the extent to which an individual's human formation is grounded in and shaped by the paschal mystery of Jesus Christ. People will look to you, their catechetical leader, as a spiritual guide—someone who understands what it means to be on the spiritual journey as a disciple of Christ. Spiritual formation is nourished by a life of prayer (including reading and praying with Scripture), a liturgical life (grounded in the celebration of the sacraments, especially the Eucharist), and the practice of empathizing with people during their moments of joy and sorrow. A catechetical leader who has core competency in spiritual formation demonstrates a hunger for holiness through practices, attitudes, and dispositions. He or she is capable of developing a spirituality sensitive to diverse cultural expressions based on conversion, communion, mission, and solidarity.

A healthy spiritual formation is manifested in a catechetical leader who exhibits an authentic relationship with Christ and the Church that is nurtured through prayer and reading of Scripture. He or she also evidences a devotion to the Eucharist and to Mary and the saints and articulates an awareness of the nearness of God in everyday living.

In order to develop these elements of spiritual formation, it is recommended that the pastoral minister engage in daily prayer and spiritual practices, spiritual direction, faith-sharing and theological reflection, the practice of justice and charity, and studying the lives of the saints.

Intellectual Formation

When you take your car to a mechanic for repairs, you trust that he or she has a good knowledge of what's under the hood and how all the various "pieces" work together to make a car run efficiently. In the same way, those people who are now looking to you for catechetical leadership expect and trust that you have a certain level of competence when it comes to knowing and being able to explain the basic principles, doctrines, and traditions of the Catholic Church. This type of formation can often be very challenging because acquiring it formally (through a certificate or a degree) involves an investment of time and money. And yet, such knowledge is crucial as you are called to make decisions that involve a solid understanding of theology, ecclesiology, Church Tradition, and catechetical theory and methodology. A catechetical leader with core competency in intellectual formation demonstrates understanding of Catholic theological studies and knowledge in ministry and an ability to know and integrate all areas of theology into ministerial practice, including Catholic social teaching, for the transformation of church and society.

Such formation must be broad enough to deepen knowledge and appreciation of the four pillars of the Catholic faith—creed, worship, morality, and prayer—as well as pastoral theology, spirituality, and Canon law. While the catechetical leader need not be a walking encyclopedia of dogmatic theology, he or she needs to exhibit a foundational understanding of Church teachings and the ability to access such information for him- or herself and for others.

Intellectual formation is developed in and through participation and engagement in small groups, lectures, discussions, course work, seminars, independent research, guided learning projects, and theological reflection.

Pastoral Formation

In many professions, it means a great deal to the rank and file if their leader is someone who has been "in the trenches" and understands the real world, rather than someone who spends too much time in an ivory tower. Pope Francis famously encouraged pastoral ministers to have the "smell of the sheep"—to be engaged in real-life situations with real people instead of just having book knowledge. The aim of pastoral formation is to help the pastoral minister learn how to effectively engage people with the gospel in various situations and circumstances. A catechetical leader with core competency in pastoral formation demonstrates a range of leadership and pastoral skills for effective ministry that enables him or her to exercise a sound practice of compassionate pastoral care.

Ultimately, pastoral ministry is about relationships. As such, the catechetical leader is called to develop in the area of pastoral formation.

Healthy pastoral formation is exhibited in the catechetical leader who is capable of praying with others and leading others in prayer, offering reflections (written or spoken) that inspire others to deepen their faith, and interacting with others, especially with those in need (which requires skills in listening and counseling). Pastoral formation also deepens one's ability to organize and collaborate effectively, something we addressed in chapter 3.

To develop these elements of pastoral formation, it is recommended that the pastoral minister not only study but also engage in practical experiences in real situations (internships, demonstrations, projects, role-playing, and completing a practicum) under the guidance of a mentor, followed by theological and personal reflection.

As you reflect upon your own skills and competencies, take a moment to look at the list below. Circle those skills and roles you think are your strength areas, and underline those you may need to develop. This is by no means an exhaustive list.

- negotiating
- meeting planning
- organization
- accuracy
- positive attitude
- collaboration
- conflict resolution
- adaptability
- counseling
- decision making
- delegating
- communication
- motivating
- multitasking

- public speaking
- recruiting
- reliability
- consistency
- achieving
- assertiveness
- empathy
- active listening
- time management
- trustworthiness
- responsibility
- commitment
- flexibility
- innovating

As you seek to build your own skills and competencies, check with your diocesan catechetical office and the National Conference for Catechetical Leadership (NCCL) for resources and programs that may help you grow in your ministry and help you find a network of colleagues who can share best practices and ideas with you.

According to a popular saying, "Great leaders are born, not made." In reality, however, while the capacity for great leadership may be innate for some people, many others need to acquire leadership skills through specialized training. In today's complex and increasingly secular world, it is crucial that we as catechetical leaders have the proper skills and core competencies to engage in the lives of the people we serve.

Professionalism in the Catechetical Ministry

We quickly learn what our core competencies are (and are not) when we are thrown into the deep end of the pool, so to speak, and begin working in a field we are interested in. When I was in college, I toyed with the idea of doing hospital ministry. Under the supervision of a very fine man, Deacon Rodriguez, I spent nearly eight months volunteering in the field of hospital ministry and learning about the core competencies needed to excel in this ministry. I personally decided that I would not be able to handle the emotional stress when people are hurting so greatly, but I also came to recognize and appreciate the need for a certain level of professionalism in ministry.

As a result, in my first job as a catechetical leader, which was in a small parish in northwest Houston, I approached my ministry with a better understanding of my own core competencies, gifts, and talents, as well as of my limitations. I also quickly came to appreciate the scope and complexity of the catechetical ministry and the fact that it required much more than a functionary to open doors, place textbooks in the classrooms, make copies of additional activities, and then wait for families to show up. I soon realized that catechetical ministry was much more than just the "program." While classes did need to be held and catechists did need to be trained, the "program" we were offering was not engaging families, and catechists viewed themselves primarily as facilitators of textbook-reading sessions. Things were definitely in "maintenance mode." Breaking the parish out of this mentality would require leadership with specific skills and specialized training.

I also learned that effectively engaging all learners at various stages of their lives in a more intimate relationship with Jesus Christ required no small amount of professionalism. In his book *Dreams and Visions* (Twenty-Third Publications, 2007, 12), Bill Huebsch discusses whole-community catechesis, which mimics certain elements of the catechumenate in order to give new life to the parish. Such an approach includes

- retreats
- small communities of growing faith
- sponsors and mentors
- liturgical experiences
- breaking open the word
- catechists formed for life
- mystagogical reflection

None of these elements could be found in the parish where I was serving as catechetical leader, so I knew that I would need training in these areas to make them happen in my parish ministry. Luckily for me, as the *National Certification Standards for Lay Ecclesial Ministers* were formulated and promulgated, I was able to begin pursuing my own professional development. This process culminated in completing a Master of Arts degree in pastoral studies from the University of Saint Thomas School of Theology at Saint Mary's Seminary in Houston, Texas.

You may or may not be in a position to pursue formal education or training at the present moment. Whatever circumstances you find yourself in, however, always be ready to take the next best step for yourself. This might mean taking a seminar, participating in a webinar, reading a book, or auditing a course. The catechetical ministry calls us to excellence, and the people of God deserve nothing less than the very best when it comes to their faith formation.

Summary: Leadership in the Twenty-First Century

"So that everyone who belongs to God may be proficient, equipped for every good work." (2 Tim. 3:17)

Catechetical ministry requires a certain level of professionalism that models the style of servant leadership Jesus exudes in the Gospels. Most important, catechetical ministry is not just a job or a profession in the strict sense of the word. Rather, by virtue of the sacrament of baptism, it is a sacred calling, a gift from God, who has invited you into this venture of forming disciples for Christ. Therefore, certain competencies, pastoral skills, and abilities are needed to ensure that you become an effective catechetical leader as God desires so that you can empower others to serve and lead as Jesus did.

For Reflection and Discussion

- How do I show professionalism in my catechetical leadership? How am I seeking to grow in my professionalism? Who or what can help me in this area?
- How do I demonstrate appreciation of and gratitude for my catechists?

Growing as a Catechetical Leader

Catechetical leadership requires a set of standards that promote credibility, stability, consistency, and excellence in lay ecclesial ministry. These standards are organized into four formation categories: human, spiritual, intellectual, and pastoral. Make a plan for developing competency in these areas. Identify areas in which you would like to grow in the coming year and the types of training that would help you do this.

Go to www.loyolapress.com/ECL to access the worksheet.

Suggested Action

Several national organizations—such as the National Conference for Catechetical Leadership (NCCL), the National Association for Lay Ministry (NALM), the Federation for Catechesis with Hispanics (FCH), and the National Federation for Catholic Youth Ministry (NFCYM)—offer opportunities at their conferences that can enhance your level of professionalism through networking, best practices, and published resources. If you are not a member, consider joining one of these organizations, and invite your catechists to do the same.

For Further Consideration

> *National Certification Standards for Lay Ecclesial Ministers.* (Alliance for the Certification of Lay Ecclesial Ministers, 2011).
>
> *Sharing Wisdom: A Process for Group Decision Making.* Mary Benet McKinney, OSB (Merrimack, NH: Thomas More Press, 1987).

Collaboration: Uniting Our Gifts in Ministry. Loughlan Sofield, ST,
    and Carroll Juliano, SHCJ (Notre Dame, IN: Ave Maria Press,
    2000).

The Promise of Partnership. Evelyn Eaton Whitehead and James D.
    Whitehead (Lincoln, NE: iUniverse, 2000).

*Co-Workers in the Vineyard of the Lord: A Resource for Guiding the
    Development of Lay Ecclesial Ministry* (Washington, D.C.:
    United States Conference of Catholic Bishops, 2005).

5

If It Takes a Village, Better Build One: Leadership and Fostering *Communio*

Encountering the Inner Life of the Trinity

No, the title of this chapter does not contain a spelling error! I wrote *communio*, not *communion*, on purpose. *Communio* is a concept that goes much deeper than an experience of unity. *Communio* is what we find and encounter in the inner life of God: Father, Son, and Holy Spirit—an intimacy so profound that the three Persons of the Trinity are one. Theologian Henri de Lubac pointed out that "the mystery of the Trinity has opened to us a totally new perspective: the ground of being is *communio*" (*La Foi Chrétienne*, Aubier, 1970, 14). As people made in the image and likeness of God—a Triune God—we are called to *communio*.

In *communio*, we truly and mysteriously become one organism, one entity, one body in Christ, and all parts of the body work together to build the kingdom. We are neither conservative nor liberal but rather *communio*. As catechetical leaders entrusted with building *communio*, our task is to recognize the internal union of God's people and to enflesh that union externally in the way we live as a church.

Take a moment to reflect on the following words of Pope Benedict XVI, who, as Prefect for the Congregation of the Doctrine of

Faith, explained that the key to understanding *communio* is Mary, the Mother of Jesus.

> The Church is not an apparatus, nor a social institution, nor one social institution among many others. It is a person. It is a woman. It is a Mother. It is alive. A Marian understanding of the Church is totally opposed to the concept of the Church as a bureaucracy or a simple organization. We cannot make the Church, we must be the Church. We are the Church, the Church is in us only to the extent that our faith more than action forges our being. Only by being Marian, can we become the Church. At its very beginning the Church was not made, but given birth. She existed in the soul of Mary from the moment she uttered her *fiat*. This is the most profound will of the Council: the Church should be awakened in our souls. Mary shows us the way. ("Ecclesiology of Vatican II," *L'Osservatore Romano*, January 23, 2002)

Communio is easier said than done, of course! In *Pensées*, French philosopher Blaise Pascal noted that "a plurality that cannot be integrated into unity is chaos; unity unrelated to plurality is tyranny" (quoted in Hans Urs von Balthasar, *The Office of Peter and the Structure of the Church* [Ignatius Press, 1974], 21). Luckily for us, the concept of *communio*, a deeply integrated plurality, is "illustrated" in the life of the early church as depicted in the Acts of the Apostles.

The Christian Community

Since the early church, groups of believers have come together to celebrate Eucharist. In the Acts of the Apostles, we are told that the earliest Christians "devoted themselves to the apostles' teaching and fellowship, to the breaking of the bread and the prayers" (Acts 2:42). In doing so, they became a new entity, a body of believers who had something in common and were united for a specific purpose. In other words, they lived *communio*. Early followers of Jesus believed and shared in the common conviction that Christ was present and that they were privileged to participate in the sacred mysteries. Jesus himself spoke of this image of community by referring to himself as the vine and his followers as the branches (John 15:5). Furthermore, Saint Paul spoke of the Mystical Body of Christ as one body with many members, united in Christ (cf. 1 Cor. 12).

Based on these very early examples and reflections, we can say that community is formed when people

- gather together
- share a common interest
- engage in communication
- share certain aspirations
- share certain norms of behavior.

In her book *Fashion Me a People,* Maria Harris describes the essence of community as a profound dream of longing and an unavoidably religious idea. "Deep within the human heart," she writes, "is a longing for a holy time when 'all will be one,' a dream of a new heaven and a new earth where death shall be no more, neither shall there be mourning nor crying nor pain anymore" (76).

Fostering *communio* is no easy task; however, it is a vital aspect of catechetical ministry that impacts how faith formation is carried out in the life of the parish. There is no catechetical program that is planned, lived, and celebrated in a vacuum. Remember, as a catechetical leader you are called to lead as Jesus did and minister to the people of your parish. Is it messy? Of course it is! You are interacting with people—with their joys, griefs, and sufferings—but you do this out of love. Therefore, it is very important that, as a catechetical leader, you initiate, nurture, and empower people of your parish to create a positive environment that fosters discipleship and builds a sense of *communio* that is inviting, warm, and inclusive of all.

When a community of people is being led in an effective way, it can be a supportive environment not just for faith formation but also for the transformation of hearts. Indeed, the goal or common interest of evangelizing groups of people is communion with one another in Christ. In the Gospel of John, Jesus teaches that love and unity are hallmarks of the Christian faith: "By this everyone will know that you are my disciples, if you have love for one another" (John 13:35). Emphasizing the love of one another in Christ, Pope Saint John Paul II said that "the definitive aim of catechesis is to put people not only in touch but in communion, in intimacy, with Jesus Christ" (*Catechesi Tradendae*, #5).

Challenges to *Communio*

In his 2002 presidential address, "The Life of the Church as Communio," then-president of the USCCB Bishop Wilton Gregory called on the church to once again embrace the notion of *communio*. In doing so, he identified three challenges that we need to overcome if we are to truly achieve the sense of *communio* that the early church exemplified.

- The first challenge, according to Bishop Gregory, is the ability "to see the mystery of God as Trinity . . . dwelling within us." Each of us is called to recognize the divine within ourselves and, as catechetical leaders, we are called to help others recognize the divine within themselves.

- The second challenge is for each of us to recognize that "my brothers and sisters in the faith are a part of me." We are one Body of Christ, "an organic blending of legitimate diversities" (Pope Saint John Paul II, *Novo Millennio Ineunte*, 46).

- The third challenge is "to move beyond the recognition of the communion we have with God and with one another and to live it"—to live with a love that is completely selfless.

According to Bishop Gregory, the *communio* that the early church experienced on Pentecost not only was our beginning but is also our destiny. Fostering *communio* as Jesus experienced it with his disciples is integral to the mission of the church; first, he surrounded himself with them and was then able to teach them how to continue building the kingdom of God by establishing a community of believers.

As catechetical leaders, we must remain cognizant that all the faithful are needed and essential to building up the entire Body of Christ. The 1980s song by Michael Jackson and Lionel Richie titled "We Are the World" puts it this way: "Let's realize that a change can only come / When we stand together as one." Isn't that what God is calling us to do—to be in communion with him through his Son, Jesus Christ, and, by doing so, to be a community of believers transformed?

Forming people into community is the task not only of the catechetical leader but of every member of the faith community—from the choir director to the volunteer in the soup kitchen ministry. All baptized members have a responsibility to give credible witness and form disciples for Christ. The *General Directory for Catechesis* states, "Catechesis is a responsibility of the entire Christian community . . . [and] 'it should not be the work of catechists and priests alone, but of the whole community of the faithful'"(#220). It goes on to say that the "Christian community is the origin, locus, and goal of catechesis. Proclamation of the Gospel always begins with the Christian community and invites [people] to conversion and the following of Christ" (#254). Within this community, there are many people who participate in the work of forming disciples, including the following: parents, godparents, sponsors, Catholic school teachers and principals, catechetical leaders, catechists, youth ministers, campus ministers, pastoral associates and other lay ecclesial ministers, women and men in consecrated life, deacons, priests, diocesan staff, bishops, and last but not least, all the baptized.

In 2015, *U.S. Catholic* published an interview with Fr. Jack Wall, president of Catholic Extension, a national fund-raising organization that supports rural dioceses with limited resources. Fr. Wall was asked how the group's contributions have led to the transformation of communities (many without priests) and how mission dioceses differ from areas where Church institutions are strong. Fr. Wall responded, "Catholic communities in mission dioceses have a sense of responsibility for the church." In these dioceses, he continued, "there's a sense of 'we're here to do God's work' . . . [and community members] own that sense of responsibility."

Wouldn't it be great if all people in our parishes became actively engaged in their faith and assumed responsibility for the mission of the church? Imagine all the people that come to Ash Wednesday services, and then imagine that you could snap your fingers and make each of those individuals take responsibility for the mission of the parish! There is no magic involved in this endeavor, however. The task begins with articulating expectations for the faithful who, by virtue of their baptism, have become not members in a club but partners in a "company"—not in the corporate sense but in the sense Saint Ignatius intended when he referred to himself and his followers as "the company of Jesus." For Ignatius, a former soldier, the word "company" meant that members of the group had both privileges and duties. As a catechetical leader, one of the keys to creating and fostering a sense of *communio* among the faithful is to place high expectations on those you serve.

The Spirituality of *Communio*

Pope Saint John Paul II presented the concept of a "spirituality of communion" in his apostolic letter *Novo Millennio Ineunte* as the basis for pastoral planning and building Catholic communities in the Church. "Before making practical plans," he writes, "we need *to promote a spirituality of communion*, making it the guiding principle of education wherever individuals and Christians are formed" (#43).

To promote such a spirituality, we must do the following:

- Seek the spiritual conversion and transformation of each believer.
- Be open to the guidance of the Holy Spirit.
- Cultivate the ability to see the positive in others.
- Commit ourselves to making room for others.
- Actively resist selfish temptations, jealousy, competition, careerism, distrust, and division.

Only by doing these things will we as catechetical leaders model the spirituality of communion Pope Saint John Paul II is calling for.

He goes further and deeper when he says that "external structures of communion will serve very little purpose. They would become mechanisms without a soul, 'masks' of communion rather than its means of expression and growth" (#43). Transforming a "mask" of communion into real communion takes time and intention. Before reaching out to your parish community and inviting them to be part of your catechetical ministry, talk to your pastor to see what spiritual opportunities are currently being offered and what kinds of opportunities might be needed. You can then allocate your resources and energy in a more efficient and appropriate way—remembering that the work of transforming a community is not yours alone.

Various Manifestations of Community

Community takes many shapes and forms. As a catechetical leader, you will be asked to relate to many of them. Let's take a look at some of the most common examples.

Family

I was fourteen years old when I lost my father to cancer. I'm the oldest of four, and my mom was very young when she became a widow. Those were tough years for me as a firstborn Hispanic male with no male figure to look up to. In the Hispanic community, there is a generational hierarchy of traits and responsibilities. The firstborn is expected to hold the greatest power and authority when making decisions, as well as responsibility for the wellness of the family when the father figure is absent. I was a teenager who had inherited a great load. But when things got really hard, my family, friends, and parish community were there for me. I am grateful to each one of them because I know that without their time, love, affection, and support, I probably would not have succeeded.

I grew up in the borderlands between El Paso and Ciudad Juárez. Every Sunday afternoon during my teenage years, my mom would take my brothers and me to spend time with my grandparents. Back then, all of my uncles and aunts lived in the same town, so they made an effort to be there every Sunday afternoon, too. By two o'clock the house was full of family members and occasionally friends who were considered part of the family. You can imagine all the conversations that took place—conversations about struggles, joys, and achievements—and all the laughter that filled the house. Everyone ate at the table and food was always plentiful. It was truly a weekly Thanksgiving celebration for us! There were all kinds of exchanges, opinions, and disagreements, but every interaction was conducted with *respeto*, or respect.

In the Hispanic community, respect is highly valued in interactions with others—especially if they are elderly people. I was taught to refer to my elders in a somewhat formal manner, using appropriate titles of respect such as *Señor* (Mr.) and *Señora* (Mrs.) and appropriate greetings such as *"Buenos días"* ("Good morning") or *"Buenas tardes"* ("Good afternoon"). Communal gatherings and exchanges among family members became a healing therapy for me. I found consolation when sharing greetings, meals, and stories. As I said, everyone had an opinion about everything, and some people tended to be more hardheaded than others, but it felt like family; we all trusted and loved one another. Occasionally, as in any family, some of the conversations got heated and turned into disputes, but when my grandfather spoke, everyone quieted himself or herself and listened. That didn't mean that everyone agreed with his opinion, either; but the value of respecting one's elders held such a high place of honor that no one was willing to violate or transgress it.

Today, family life is more complex, and our understanding of family is rapidly changing. However, the family still remains the most basic form of community. As a catechetical leader, one of the most powerful things you can do is to strengthen and nourish families so that they can experience *communio* in the home, the domestic church. Our parishes, and our faith-formation programs in particular, need to be more family friendly if we are going to have any hope of fostering a spirit of *communio*.

School Community

Before my father died, we lived in Portland, Oregon, for a short time. When we moved there, everything was new to us. And I mean everything: customs, language, culture, friends, home, lifestyle, you name it. Nevertheless, I found my Hosford Middle School teachers and peers to be inclusive. Even though I was a complete stranger, the school personnel and my new friends made the place feel like home. This beautiful school community valued friendship, sincerity, and openness to learning from one other, and these values made it special. My teachers and friends knew my limitations and still honored me for who I was. I was never questioned or challenged but rather embraced and recognized as one of them.

I believe this is the kind of *encuentro*, or encounter, that Pope Francis often speaks of. It is what I call the ministry of presence. No matter what our race, ethnicity, socioeconomic status, or preferences may be, we are all children of God and loved by him. The Golden Rule states that we should treat one another as we wish to be treated (Luke 6:31). Community life can be strengthened when we treat others with respect and kindness. Whether through your parish school, faith-formation program, or both, you have an opportunity to influence the extent to which a sense of *communio* is fostered.

Parish Community

As we grew accustomed to life in Portland, church became our second home. The beauty of our Catholic faith is that no matter how far you are from home, the common beliefs, prayers, practices, rituals, and liturgies are always available to help you reaffirm your identity as a Christian. I don't remember exactly when St. Patrick's and the national shrine The Grotto became our places of worship, but they were without a doubt sanctuaries for my family. I remember going to Spanish Mass at St. Patrick's one Sunday morning, and the ushers greeted us right from the start, noticing we were new members and doing what they could to make us feel at home. People from other ministries were very welcoming too. When they learned that my father was sick, they offered to help my mother with everyday tasks such as taking my father to his medical appointments. Surely members of this parish were living out their baptismal call; they paid full attention to everyone who walked through their doors.

What gifts and resources did these two communities offer to my family that made an impact? Here are just a few of them.

- a welcoming attitude
- hospitality
- openness
- respect
- acceptance
- Mass offered in Spanish

- social services
- music

- youth engagement
- a caring pastor

These elements made St. Patrick's and The Grotto thriving communities because they enabled parishioners to reach out and intentionally connect—person to person and family to family.

Our Parish Communities Are Changing

Several years ago, a project known as Emerging Models of Pastoral Leadership was undertaken with the intention of examining areas of pastoral excellence and promoting models of pastoral leadership while identifying the current challenges of parish life and framing a vision of how to respond effectively. In one book of the series that emerged from this project, *Shaping Catholic Parishes* (Carole Ganim, ed., Loyola Press, 2008), a number of priests, deacons, and lay ministers share their experiences as pastoral leaders in situations of five types: welcoming, collaboration, ethical, pastoral, and prophetic. At the end of the book, Sr. Donna Markham, OP, PhD, offers a reflection from a psychologist's point of view. She expresses the opinion that communities large and small respond positively or negatively to the pathologies, or weaknesses, of its leaders. She concludes by posing three questions that are essential to consider when attempting to foster *communio*.

1. Whose parish is it?
2. Who has authority to make decisions?
3. How will conflicts be resolved?

We will explore each of these three questions in the following chapters.

Summary: Carry Each Other's Burdens

"Carry each other's burdens, and in this way you will fulfill the law of Christ." (Gal. 6:2, NIV)

It is important to remember that the parish is nothing at all like a "filling station" where people come to get refueled. A filling station is a self-serve, individualistic experience. Our parish, and in particular the faith-formation program, must be a place where true encounter occurs and where relationships are fostered. Saint Paul urges followers of Christ to "carry each other's burdens"—to live not for ourselves but for one another and for the common good. This is at the heart of what it means to have a spirit of *communio*: to share in the unity that is found in the life of the Trinity—three Persons in such intimate relationship that they are one. Each faith community must have a sense of openness and caring for people at all stages of their faith journey. No one individual or group can do it alone: it takes a whole village to raise a child, and it takes the entire parish community to make disciples.

For Reflection and Discussion

- As a parish catechetical leader, what values do I bring to my parish?
- How do I give life to the parish community and foster a sense of *communio*?

Growing as a Catechetical Leader

Building a community requires a contribution from every baptized member of a parish. As we have discussed, it is the responsibility of the whole community to form disciples. Begin by assessing the strengths of your parish community. Make a list of them, and share it with the rest of the parish. Later, annotate what areas of your parish life could be enhanced. Go to www.loyolapress.com/ECL to access the worksheet.

Suggested Action

Talk to your parish pastoral council and seek ways for the leaders of various ministries to brainstorm how to form disciples and foster a sense of *communio*.

For Further Consideration

The General Directory for Catechesis. (Washington, DC: United States Conference of Catholic Bishops, 1998).

"Building Dynamic Faith Communities in Surprising Places: An Interview with Father Jack Wall, the President of Catholic Extension," *U.S. Catholic*, July 2015, www.uscatholic.org/articles/201507/building-dynamic-faith-communities-surprising-places-30237.

Novo Millennio Ineunte. Pope John Paul II (Rome: Libreria Editrice Vaticana, 2001).

Shaping Catholic Parishes: Pastoral Leaders in the 21st Century.
  Carole Ganim, ed., Emerging Models of Pastoral Leadership
  (Chicago: Loyola Press, 2008).

Fashioning a People Today: The Educational Insights of Maria Harris.
  Gabriel Moran (New London, CT: Twenty-Third
  Publications, 2007).

6

Let No One Disregard You: Leadership and Legitimate Authority

Says Who?

If you watch children interact for any amount of time, before long you will witness a conflict in which one child challenges another:

"Hey, that's *my* chair!"
"Oh, yeah? Says who?"
"Says me!"

And so on.

The funny thing is, we never really outgrow the tendency to ask the question, "Says who?" It is in our nature to question authority. When Jesus spoke publicly, he was questioned by the scribes and Pharisees. "By what authority are you doing these things?" they asked. "And who gave you authority to do this?" (Mark 11:28, NIV). In essence, they were asking Jesus, "Says who?" Jesus, of course, left no doubt that all authority comes from the Father. What astonished people, however, was Jesus' revelation that he and the Father are one (John 10:30)—which means that he shares the Father's authority. In fact, Jesus made it quite clear that "all authority in heaven and on earth has been given to me" (Matt. 28:18). For our purposes, we need to pay close attention to how Jesus understood authority and what he did with it.

As we said, Jesus asserted that all authority had been given to him. He, in turn, entrusted this authority to Peter and the Apostles. "I tell you, you are Peter, and on this rock I will build my church, and the gates of Hades will not prevail against it. I will give you the keys of the kingdom of heaven, and whatever you bind on earth will bound in heaven, and whatever you loose on earth will be loosed in heaven" (Matt. 16:18–19).

So, let's follow the "paper trail" of authority.

- All authority comes from God, the author of life.
- The Father has given all authority to Jesus.
- Jesus entrusted his authority to Peter and the Apostles.
- The bishops are the successors of the Apostles.
- The bishops have entrusted pastors with this authority.
- The pastor, in the name of the bishop, is entrusting you with a share in this authority.

Suffice it to say, you *do* have a position of authority within the Church—an authority that is of divine origin and entrusted to human heads, hearts, and hands. So when people challenge your authority and ask, "Says who?" in response to a decision you have made or a policy you are promulgating, be sure to cite your sources of authority: the pastor, the bishop, Peter and the Apostles, Jesus, and the Father himself! You do not own this authority, but you have a share in it, must exercise it properly, and are accountable for it.

Authority and the Ability to Influence

When I was in fourth grade, I had a classmate named Gustavo, but everyone knew him as "Tavo." Tavo was the tallest and biggest kid in the classroom, and because of his size, he was intimidating. And yet he was not a bully. Tavo was a loyal friend and a defender of any kid who was being bullied. He actually tried to keep everyone at peace. He was one of the nicest kids I had ever met—and he exhibited a sense of authority. For that reason, my earliest understanding of authority was linked to physical strength and power that was used to influence others. While Tavo exercised his authority well, it soon became clear to me that authority based on physical strength could easily lead to an abuse of power and subordination of others if not done for the service of others and in a positive way.

Eventually, I learned that power means the ability to influence others either positively *or* negatively. While frequently construed as negative, power in itself is merely a capacity to act. Some may see all power as evil and corrupt, but in fact, power can influence decisions toward good actions. Christians need not fear the word *power* since Jesus uses the Greek word *dunamis* (meaning "power") to describe the essence of the Holy Spirit: "I am going to send you what my Father has promised; but stay in the city until you have been clothed with power from on high" (Luke 24:49, NIV). In this sense, the power of influence can be understood as the ability to inspire and motivate others to follow a certain goal.

For many of us, the first example we have of such power and authority is our parents. In my case, my father wasn't so much a rule enforcer but instead had many of the qualities of a right-brained person: he was warm, highly social, and possessed great charisma, which naturally attracted others. My mother, on the other hand, was more of a left-brained person: she was driven by logic, discipline, and reason. Certainly, I inherited personal traits from both of them and unconsciously imitate those traits. Their power of influence wasn't forced on me; it just naturally got engrained in me. Their sense of humor and intellectual curiosity and my father's ability to socialize with anyone and everyone make me who I am. Their good examples in both word and deed had a power of influence on my decision-making style, my life perspectives, and the values I hold.

Beyond my parents, there was a community of people, including catechists, schoolteachers, and older adults, who had a positive influence on me as role models, especially in the area of exercising authority. One of my teachers, Mr. Ruben, taught me the value of friendship and honesty and insisted that everyone was capable of earning good grades. I don't recall anyone in his class feeling down or unhappy. Mr. Ruben truly inspired his students to do better, and his authority was never questioned—not because of his physical strength, but because of his inherent moral character and virtue. Not everyone, however, is capable of exuding such a natural sense of authority. Let's take a look at the reasons why.

How Does Power Work?

As previously mentioned, power is the capacity and ability to get things done. In their article "Are There No Limits to Authority?" David Knights and Darren McCabe explain that "it is erroneous to ask who has power. Instead, it is necessary to explore how power is exercised" (*Organization Studies*, March 22, 1999). People in leadership roles are able to influence the behavior of others to achieve some goals or objectives. Take, for instance, the civil rights leader Dr. Martin Luther King Jr. and the cult leader David Koresh. Both men had the capacity to influence and change the behavior of their followers. However, the former did so in a positive way, while the latter did so in a tragically negative way (leading numerous people to their deaths at the standoff in Waco, Texas, in 1993).

Power, therefore, is simply the ability to create action. According to social psychologists John R. P. French Jr. and Bertram Raven, there are five bases of power.

- Legitimate—the belief that a person has the formal right to make demands and expect others to be obedient
- Reward—the ability to compensate another for compliance
- Expert—the possession of knowledge, skills, or information that others need
- Referent—charisma, perceived attractiveness, and a sense of being worthy and having a right to others' respect
- Coercive—the belief that one can punish others for noncompliance (*Studies in Social Power*. Dorwin Cartwright, ed. [Ann Arbor: University of Michigan Press, 1959], 155–165).

In the context of leadership, these five bases of power can be reduced to two.

1. Personal, or referential, power—possessing the personality traits, expertise, charisma, and persuasive skills needed to influence others
2. Legitimate, or official, power—possessing the right to influence others based on one's position or authority

As a catechetical leader, you may possess personal or referential power, meaning that you may have certain innate qualities, skills, virtues, and traits that inspire or influence others to follow you. Think of it as charisma. In your role as a catechetical leader, you have also been imbued with "legitimate power," which is the kind that comes with a position of authority. Authority and power are intertwined: power is the ability to create action, while authority is the foundation on which that power is built. The key to successful servant leadership is the ability to use referential power and legitimate power together, not for personal glory or honor but for the service of others in a way that influences positive behavior for the building of the kingdom of God, while at the same time respecting and honoring the integrity of the human person.

Legitimate Power

The most common type of power a catechetical leader has is known as legitimate power, or "positional power." This type of power derives from your position of leadership within the structures of Church hierarchy. Volunteers, catechists, and other people in the Church rightly see you as someone with the authority to direct their actions. For example, a group of catechists may approach you to tell you that because the month of October—the month of the holy rosary—is coming up, it might be appropriate to substitute one of the scheduled lessons with an opportunity to pray the Rosary as a community. They recognize that you have legitimate power to approve or deny their request. Regardless of your decision, they understand that they must comply.

For anyone who has it, however, there is the danger of abusing positional power for personal honor and glory without meeting or serving the needs of others. Doing so places a person in what can be thought of as "pedestal leadership." In other words, a leader with either referential or legitimate power who has no intention of serving others is more of a ruler than a leader. On the other hand, as Robert Greenleaf explains, servant leaders are able to exercise power and authority successfully because they live by their conscience—because a certain set of values (including respect, honesty, kindness, trust, and sincerity) guides the execution of their role. When a leader and follower both subscribe to these values, a reciprocal relationship of mutual respect is likely to develop.

Power of influence can also be understood as reward power, which comes from the ability to create positive incentives or external motivation through some sort of promotion that does not require positional power. Coercive power, on the other hand, is the opposite of reward power. Coercive leaders punish their followers for not meeting their expectations. This can be done through psychological manipulation, passive-aggressive put-downs, or even physical force. This type of leadership stands in contrast to the "persuasive power of Jesus, who is convincing when he simply tells his disciples, 'Follow me'" (Dan Ebener, *Servant Leadership Models for Your Parish*, 8).

Coercive Power

Several years ago I was doing a presentation for a group of pastoral ministers. At the end of the day, a couple came up to me and related that the volunteer leader of their lay ecclesial movement was manipulating the movement for the sake of profit and his own reputation. This charismatic leader regularly asked for large donations of money and forced team members to adhere to rigid and unrealistic rules and guidelines. If anyone contested or disagreed with him, it was like disobeying God. This type of coercive power instills fear, suppresses free will, manipulates conscience, and corrodes critical thinking. How can someone exercise Christian leadership and still get away with such coercive behavior? Unfortunately, it happens far too often. This particular ministry had evolved into a cult, and its attitudes and practices had spread to a neighboring diocese. Thankfully, word reached diocesan leaders, and the person was removed from his role.

The lesson of this story is that as catechetical leaders, we need to be aware of this type of leadership style and know that it may materialize in any one of our colleagues—a superior, a coworker, or a volunteer—or even in ourselves. While we may think that we are immune to this temptation, Paulo Freire reminds us that "it is a rare peasant who, once promoted to overseer, does not become more of a tyrant towards his former comrades than the owner himself" (Paulo Freire, *Pedagogy of the Oppressed*, 46).

Referential Power

When I was a very young man, I got into a fight with my brother and got punished by being forced to attend a strange party alone with my mom. As we walked the very short distance from our own home, I anticipated seeing children swinging joyfully at a piñata. Instead, as we entered the house, I saw a group of moms—some perusing catalogs, others eating salads, and still others standing around a big table where plastic containers of all sizes and colors were displayed for them to see. You have probably guessed by now what kind of punishment party my mother took me to: a Tupperware party. Our neighbor had become a consultant and turned out to be very good at selling. Within a week, my mother had three salad bowls, and within a month, my maternal grandmother revealed her own collection of containers. Within two months, pretty much the entire block had Tupperware products in their homes. My neighbor influenced people not by her position but by inspiring other women to believe that her product was the best on the market and there was nothing else like it.

As catechetical leaders, given the authority and position granted us by the Church, we sometimes sell ourselves short and forget how to influence others by inspiring them to follow the incredible good news of Jesus Christ! Don't get me wrong: in no way am I comparing Jesus Christ to a product. However, as a leader in ministry, you must rely on inspiration, tactics, and strategies, just as the Tupperware lady did. You are reading this book because you happen to hold the positional power that comes with your role in ministry. But what if there were no positional role, no legitimate power given to you by the authority? What type of leadership style would you employ to draw people to Christ?

Referential power is based on charisma and the interpersonal skills or abilities of the leader, including the art of persuasion. Because it comes from within, it has an authentic quality, and so it inspires loyalty, trust, and respect among followers. If a leader leads by example (servant leadership) and empowers the follower to take initiative, then the follower feels inspired and is likely to take initiative with passion and creativity and, in turn, spread the passion to others. There are certain leaders who have a kind of charisma that we might consider a special gift from God. Charismatic leaders can be very charming and attractive because they have a gift of articulating a vision for the future; they have the rhetoric to influence listeners; and they often have a solution to a crisis. Charismatic leaders who know how to empower others to serve others—rather than their own interests—are on the path of servant leadership.

As a catechetical leader, consider the following strategies for exercising your authority effectively:

- **Communicate your intentions, goals, and desires clearly.** Authority is ineffective when ambiguity reigns.

- **Make yourself approachable.** Real authority does not need to hide behind a curtain as the "Wizard" of Oz did. Make sure that communication is fostered and that people are encouraged to come to you, especially when in need of help.

- **Be responsive.** Authority is increased when quick action is taken—not impulsively, but promptly, especially when responding to an inquiry or a problem. Putting people off undermines your authority and causes morale problems.

- **Encourage discussion of "failures."** Real authority seeks to help people grow, and that won't happen if people are fearful of making a mistake.

- **Don't shy away from crises.** A crisis can be an opportunity to grow as a leader and to build confidence and trust in followers. Don't shy away from crises; instead, "run toward the fire."

- **Avoid raising your voice.** Real authority does not rely on screaming and yelling, which only cause a loss of respect. Work the problem, keep it impersonal, use a calm but firm voice, and gather all the facts before jumping to a conclusion.

- **Try "lateral" leadership.** Instead of the "command and control" approach ("Everybody follow me!"), consider a "lateral" approach. Such an approach encourages building coalitions, negotiating, consulting, and networking.

- **Build relationships.** Effective authority makes connections with people, forges alliances, and nurtures relationships. Continually work to increase your sphere of influence.

- **Raise your level of expertise.** At every turn, work to increase your credibility—not to flaunt it but to reassure others that you do have expertise in the area of faith formation.

- **Be transparent.** Avoid keeping secrets and withholding information. Seek always to share information broadly and appropriately.

Jesus Taught with Authority

In the Gospel of Matthew we are told that people were astonished by the way Jesus taught and spoke of the things of the kingdom of God. "Now when Jesus had finished saying these things, the crowds were astounded at his teaching, for he taught them as one having authority, and not as their scribes" (Matt. 7:28–29). Jesus' teaching on the kingdom is radical and so new that it is compelling. His legitimate authority is not surrounded by regulations and demands as the scribes' and Pharisees' is. The scribes' teaching method was to quote various authorities before presenting their own interpretation as a synthesis, but Jesus told stories and went directly to the core of the question with his own interpretation. Jesus also cared more about people than about rules and regulations. This is the spirit of leadership that we are called to bring to the catechetical ministry.

So how are we to lead with authority and not become authoritarians or imposing rulers? The answer lies in the capacity and measure of how we love one another as Jesus expects us to love (Matt. 22:36–40). In fact, love is "the ultimate measure" (Ebener, *Servant Leadership Models for Your Parish*, 4) and the visible, concrete sign that people should see in the lives and communities of our parishes. Love at its core is free and not arrogant; it is kind and merciful, undemanding, unimposing, and it does not glorify itself.

Jesus' authority and power flowed from his radical love and compassion for others. It is only love that is able to modify and shape certain behaviors and lifestyles of the follower. He gave excellent teachings to his disciples about how to exercise his style of leadership and still lead with authority: "Whoever wants to be first must be last of all and servant of all" (Mark 9:35). He taught them to build the kingdom of God using the "tools" provided in the Beatitudes (Matt. 5:3–12). Jesus served others by focusing on the needs of others and not his own. He lived and demonstrated what he practiced and taught even to the point of his death (Luke 23:34). Jesus' heart was a servant heart, and he exhibited integrity and consistency between what he taught and what he practiced.

People see you, the catechetical leader, in a position of power. You might not have asked for it, but there you are. You have probably noticed that people are always seeking you out for guidance. There will be times when you may feel overwhelmed and want to be alone and not to be bothered, or times when you feel uneasy about how to direct people. Whatever the situation may be, don't allow yourself to become discouraged. Rather, embrace your call. Remember that you have been asked to lead people to God, not to rule over them. If you need to take a breather, do so. There is nothing wrong with taking time for yourself; even Jesus went out to pray in solitude to reenergize for the following day (Mark 1:35). Leading people is a complex task and requires patience and a strong dose of compassion—for others and for yourself.

Whether you are new to your role or already leading people, take a pause and reevaluate your style of leadership by answering the following questions:

- What can I do to enable my catechists or others to achieve their full potential?
- How can I better reflect Christ's love by treating others with respect and compassion?
- Does my style of leadership show concern for the interests of others?
- Does my style of leadership encourage others in their call as disciples of Christ?
- Does my style of leadership delegate important responsibilities with a negative attitude or imposing manner?
- Does my style of leadership emphasize the importance of giving back to the community?

Power, authority, and influence can best be summarized by the following Bible passage:

"Let your light shine before others, that they may see your good deeds and glorify your Father in heaven" (Matt. 5:16, NIV).

Honor the Past

In 2007, the longtime owner of the Chicago Blackhawks hockey team, William Wirtz, passed away. For many years Wirtz ran the club with an iron fist and had policies that were unpopular with many fans (such as not showing home games on local TV). Upon his passing, he was succeeded by his son, Rocky Wirtz, who immediately announced that there were going to be changes in the way the team was run. However, he did not throw his late father "under the bus" in order to satisfy long-suffering fans. Instead, he honored his father and said he had done what he thought was right for the team and the fans, but he also said it was time to move on. Changes were made (including broadcasting home games on local TV) but without burning bridges to the past.

In your role as a catechetical leader, be aware of one misstep that many leaders make unintentionally and that adversely affects their authority: expressing contempt for what or who preceded you. When a leader is new to a position, it is not uncommon for that leader to want to make an impression by heralding new plans and directions. While there is nothing wrong with setting a new course, it is often done at the expense of a previous course of action or direction that some people may have found valuable and continue to hold dear. The best course of action to solidify your authority is to honor that which has gone before you, point out where it has brought people thus far, and explain how it is time now to build on that legacy. Changes need not be seen as a repudiation of the past. As a catechetical leader, you can shoot yourself in the foot by bad-mouthing a predecessor and/or his or her choice of textbook, format, procedures, policies, or practices. In doing so, you may alienate some of the very people you need to rely on going forward. Rather, honor the past and build a sense of continuity that communicates to people that you see yourself as part of a tradition—*their* tradition.

Summary: The Power of Service

"Whoever serves me, the Father will honor." (John 12:26)

As catechetical leaders, our authentic power is used in the service of the Lord and relies on the capacity and measure of how we love our neighbor as Jesus expects each one of us to love. This authority, given by the Church, should not be abused or unleashed in a dictatorial or authoritarian way. Rather, it should be exercised in a spirit of service that helps others become credible witnesses to the teachings of the Lord.

For Reflection and Discussion

- How do you lead others? Do you command by demanding or by inviting?
- When it comes to leadership, what behavioral traits can you learn from Jesus of Nazareth?

Growing as a Catechetical Leader

Working with people who have different agendas can be overwhelming. It can be difficult to find a way to lead them to the Lord. In the Mexican culture, there is a saying: "*a gritos y a sombrerazos.*" This means that when things get tough, simply roll up your sleeves and give yourself those "waves of the hat" and "shouts of encouragement" to accomplish a goal. Never forget that you are in your ministry to walk with people in the different stages of their lives, not by manipulating or controlling them but by showing them tenderness and care.

Go to www.loyolapress.com/ECL to access the worksheet.

Suggested Action

As you prepare for your day, go to the nearest mirror. Stand quietly for a few minutes and ask yourself, *Do my facial expressions match my words? When I'm not speaking, what does my face or nonverbal language say to those around me? Do I like what I see? Do I see Jesus in myself?*

For Further Consideration

French and Raven's Five Forms of Power, www.mindtools.com/pages/article/newLDR_56.htm.

The Art and Science of Leadership. Afsaneh Nahavandi (London: Pearson Education Ltd, 2014).

Just Ministry. Richard Gula (Mahwah, NJ: Paulist Press, 2010).

7

Getting to Know the Terrain: Leadership in a Changing Landscape

The End of the Catholic "Bubble"

In a bygone era, many U.S. Catholics huddled together in close-knit communities that can be likened to Catholic "ghettos," or what I like to call "Catholic bubbles." The culture in these communities "oozed" Catholicism. Structures were in place to keep the bubble intact: a homogeneous community, strong traditional families, the practice of Catholic traditions and devotions, Church leadership that went unquestioned, and low-cost Catholic schools that were affordable to most, if not all, families. Growing up in the Catholic bubble was like being marinated in Catholicism—it soaked into the very fiber of your being. One was formed as a Catholic by the family and the community practicing its way of life. All that was needed to seal the deal was for a child to learn his or her catechism—usually in the form of the *Baltimore Catechism*, a resource that used a question-and-answer format to pass on the basic doctrines and teachings of the Catholic Church.

Today, the Catholic bubble has burst. It no longer exists. Communities are much more pluralistic, and people are much more mobile. Families are experiencing great pressures and challenges. Many

Catholic traditions and devotions have gone by the wayside. In the wake of the clergy sex-abuse crisis, Church leadership has lost credibility. And, finally, rising costs have resulted in Catholic education being out of reach for many.

In many ways, however, we are still approaching faith formation with an attitude and an apparatus that were shaped in the previous century: "Leave your child with us for a few hours a week, and we'll return a fully formed Catholic to you!" You and I know that this no longer works. As a catechetical leader, your role is to keep your fingers on the pulse of this rapidly changing world while considering new formats, structures, and approaches for transmitting the good news of Jesus Christ in the most effective manner possible.

Changing Times

Observers noticed a startling difference between pictures taken in Saint Peter's Square less than eight years apart. In 2005, at the funeral of Saint Pope John Paul II, the crowds in the square are looking straight ahead, hands at their sides. In 2013, at the election of Pope Francis, almost everyone in the square is holding up a mobile device to record the moment or to take a picture. Technology is rapidly changing the way we live and interact with one another and with our world. This is why it is so crucial that as a catechetical leader you have the ability to recognize and identify patterns that may affect faith formation positively or negatively. This will help you adjust your model of delivery or change strategies according to the present reality of your parish or environment. In other words, you must adapt to serve people's needs—and not expect them to adapt to your way of doing things.

In 2012, the Catholic Conference of New York State published a statement that described the many needs and challenges of parishes and invited parish catechetical leaders to renew their commitment to the call they received. These challenges have become lived experiences across the nation, and I mention a few of them here.

- Decreased participation of children and youth in faith-formation programs
- A waning participation in Sunday Eucharist
- Priests with multiple roles, especially in merged or combined parishes
- Fewer vocations to ordained ministry
- Growing numbers of foreign priests, who make up for the lack of local priests and must struggle with various social barriers to do so
- The rise of secularism
- Rapid growth of technology
- Loss of respect for and trust in the Church due to sexual-abuse scandal
- Different types of families, from cross-generational to never married

It is crucial that as a catechetical leader you learn how to scrutinize the "signs of the times and [interpret] them in the light of the Gospel" (*Gaudium et Spes*, #4). This means that you must deeply understand the environment in which you live and its joys, sufferings, and misfortunes. The skill of scrutinizing the past, present, and projected future of your community is known as "contextualizing." It is the art of looking for patterns that may shine light on the current situation and enhance your ability to make confident decisions and effect changes in processes or programs as needed.

Catechetical ministry is contextual and relational. As I said earlier, faith formation does not take place in a vacuum but rather in a community of believers. In the Gospels, we are told that Jesus had to take his disciples aside and explain the parables to them. When his disciples asked why he spoke to the people in parables, he answered, "To you it has been given to know the secrets of the kingdom of heaven, but to them it has not been given" (Matt. 13:11). It is interesting that Jesus, knowing his audience, included in his parables common elements of the time such as wheat, seed, yeast, and so on. He didn't go about using alien concepts that people would not be able to understand. Instead, he used familiar, everyday objects that people could in some fashion relate to.

Think of what would happen today if we were to share parables using cultural phenomena that most people understand or have a sense of—the Super Bowl, Google, LeBron James, Facebook, Superman, Skype, Beyoncé, and Twitter, for example. The bottom line is that the message of the gospel needs to connect with people's lives and meet them where they are so they can come to see how God is present in their daily living. As a catechetical leader, it is imperative that you "speak the language" of those you serve so that they recognize a connection between the gospel and their everyday lives.

Casting Your Nets on the Other Side of the Boat

In his book *Reimagining Faith Formation for the 21st Century*, John Roberto presents numerous challenges to consider when running a catechetical program for all ages and generations, not the least of which are dramatic changes in family life.

Whereas the traditional family consisted of a mom, a dad, and biological children, today's families may include the following:

- Blended households
- An unmarried couple with children
- An unmarried couple without children
- A same-sex couple with children

- A same-sex couple without children
- Grandparents and parents with children
- Grandparents as primary caregivers of children
- Parents with single young adults living at home
- Single parents with young children

Paying attention to current changes in family configurations implies a willingness to let go of old structures, models, and ways of thinking that do not align with or respond to the current needs of people. It is possible that you have a sense of the rapidly changing terrain of your parish and have tried different models with only limited success. You may be doubtful that any model will work.

The Gospel of John can help us appreciate that even Simon had his doubts. When he and the other disciples have caught no fish, Jesus tells them, "Throw your net on the right side of the boat and you will find some" (John 21:6, NIV)—even though they had already been fishing for a while, to no avail. You may wonder, *Who exactly is the expert here?* Simon had been a fisherman for a number of years, and, according to the Bible, Jesus was not in the fishing business but that of carpentry.

Nevertheless, Simon agrees and decides to throw his net on the other side. As a result, the disciples "were unable to haul the net in because of the large number of fish" (John 21:6, NIV). Jesus didn't say, "Listen, Simon, it's your way of casting a net that just isn't working" or "Go and get a new set of nets because you will need them!" Simon uses what he has on hand—literally—and is willing to try what Jesus suggests, although he is skeptical that it will work.

Likewise, the key to success as a catechetical leader is to be innovative, willing to take risks, and willing to adapt to change, but to stay faithful to the message of the gospel at the same time.

Assessing the Need

The challenges present today are shaping how society is formed, how relationships are made, and how new structures or behaviors are practiced. Understanding these dynamics is a part of getting to know your terrain. As a catechetical leader, you are called to lead like Jesus and be pastorally sensitive to present realities. The following story illustrates this.

Natalia (not her real name) was hired to be the director of religious education for a midsize parish of 1300 households, 80 to 85 percent of which were Hispanic. Natalia was young, had a master's degree in theology from a prestigious theological school, was fully bilingual (English-Spanish), and was passionate about her faith, but she had little experience working as a catechetical leader. Within the first few months she realized that most parents in her program were lacking knowledge of the basic tenets of the Catholic faith, didn't know how to read Scripture, couldn't recite basic prayers, and were unfamiliar with other practices and beliefs of the Catholic faith. Natalia decided to offer faith-formation classes for parents while their children were in their own sessions. Natalia and her team spent almost two months publicizing these classes at Masses, in meetings with parents, through e-mail blasts and letters, and so on. Classes began and they were full, attended by more than 130 parents on Sunday morning for one hour and thirty minutes. The format of the class was a short welcome by one of the catechists followed by praise and worship, teaching, and finally fellowship. What could possibly go wrong?

Within a few weeks, participation had dropped drastically from 130 to 25 parents. What happened? I offered to assist Natalia and had a chance to observe the proceedings firsthand. I quickly realized that the actual content was great; it was faithful to the Magisterium of the Church, and it was solid, so I knew that wasn't the source of the parents' waning interest. Next, I decided to pay a visit to the parish and get a sense of what else might be going on. I soon learned that the parochial vicar had received an offer from several parishioners who happened to be immigration lawyers to provide free orientation workshops to the parish for a period of six weeks on Tuesday nights and Sunday mornings. The workshops were focused on DAPA (Deferred Action for Parents of Americans) and DACA (Deferred Action for Childhood Arrivals). As you can guess, many of the parents had chosen to attend these workshops. These parents had an essential need that Natalia and her staff didn't know about and never bothered to ask about. It wasn't that these parents were not interested in learning about their faith, it was that something more pressing needed to be attended to and was being provided. Lesson learned: faith formation must take into consideration the basic needs of people.

I share this story to emphasize how the experience helped Natalia understand the need to keep her finger on the pulse of her parish community. The failure of the adult-formation sessions could have been prevented if Natalia had more deeply explored the dynamics of her parish landscape.

Top Ten Implications

All of the changes in society that we have talked about in this chapter have implications for how you are to proceed as a catechetical leader in this millennium. Here are just a few of the ways that you are being called to drop your nets on the other side of the boat.

1. Because Catholic life is no longer anchored by a Catholic home or a Catholic neighborhood to the extent it once was, you will need to a) focus on ways of mobilizing the parish community to form others in faith while empowering parents to embrace their role as their children's primary educators and b) not just strengthen the domestic church but also teach parents how to build and sustain it.

2. Because families are no longer marching lockstep to the traditional way of doing faith formation and the sacraments (infant baptism, first Eucharist around second grade, confirmation between the eighth and twelfth grades, and so on), you will need to have more of a catechumenal approach to faith formation and less of an academic/grade-level one.

3. Because people are experiencing such a disconnect between their faith and everyday living, you will need to focus attention on making stronger connections between the good news of Jesus and healing the brokenness and woundedness of people's lives.

4. Because the current generation is accustomed to learning and engaging digitally, you will need to ensure that technology is fully integrated into your faith-formation formats.

5. Because a large number of the people you are called to serve have little or no understanding of the Catholic faith and its teachings and traditions, you will need to embrace the New Evangelization and engage in more robust pre-evangelization that invites people to consider entering into a relationship with Jesus and the Church and requires you to listen more intently to people's stories.

6. Because of the loss of trust resulting from the clergy sex-abuse scandal, you will need to work constantly to restore trust and credibility by emphasizing works of mercy and justice that put our faith into action and by highlighting personal witness so that people meet and hear from authentic disciples of Christ.

7. Because fewer adults have sufficient knowledge of their own faith, you will need to ramp up adult faith formation and, in particular, catechist formation and make them both absolute priorities.

8. Because of the complexity and busyness of people's lives as well as the rise of secularism, you will not be able to sit back and wait

for people to come to you; you will need to identify ways to go out to them. Evangelization will become a way of life for you and your program.

9. Because of the pluralism of our society, you will need to focus on enculturation, ecumenism, and interreligious dialogue more intentionally, proactively, and robustly than was necessary in the past.

10. Because of limited and shrinking resources, you will be called on to do more with less—which means that collaborative ministry with neighboring parishes will be nonnegotiable.

This is by no means an exhaustive list, but I don't want to frighten you away from this wonderful ministry by making the challenges seem overwhelming! It is crucial, however, that you go into this ministry with eyes wide open and with a willingness to drop your nets on the other side of the boat in order to increase your "catch."

Reality Checkup

My experience in Houston has been that for a number of years, the city has been improving their highways, roads, and drainage systems. Several years ago, the Texas Department of Transportation published an analysis of the one hundred most congested roadways in the state of Texas. It turns out that Interstate 610, which I live only a few blocks away from, has more than 1,100,000 annual hours of delay per mile and has become the number-one congested road in the entire state. Further down the list, the third most congested road is US Highway 59, also within a few blocks of my home. No wonder it takes me so long to get to work!

So what do roads and mobility performance have to do with catechetical leadership? The answer is simple: As you prepare to set up your program with calendars, meeting times with parents, sacramental sessions for reconciliation and first Eucharist, adult confirmation, catechist-training days, etc., know your families and their "traffic pat-terns" like a driver needs to know the roads! Be sure you are familiar with the infrastructure of your parish and are aware of roadblocks and challenges that can prevent you from reaching your intended destina-tion. Take time to study the demographics of your parish. If you were to take a snapshot of the life of your parish, what would you see? Who is on the periphery? Who is cropped out? What's lacking? What cen-tral events of your parish community will engage different age groups and intergenerational communities?

Before they begin a major construction project, civil engineers, city planners, surveyors, and property developers must carefully study their terrain, survey the land, and collect and assess pertinent data. For example, my brother Alan has been a civil engineer for many years in the state of Texas. Until recently, I had no idea that such a position includes planning and design in both the public and private sectors, from transportation to land development and from traffic engineering to construction management. He gathers information from surveyors that details the exact location, boundaries, and geographical features of a property and then generates plans, designs, and estimates for poten-tial investors. In other words, he is part of his company's visioning process. His employers know they can trust him to obtain data, analyze costs, and assess the type of investment a client is willing to make. This is a form of getting to know one's terrain.

Catechetical leaders are also called to survey their parish and min-istries rather than coming up with hasty solutions that are expected to meet needs but only result in hitting roadblocks. A true servant leader creates a culture of intentionality—of meeting people, getting to know their needs, and being willing to serve those needs before serving his or her own. As you do an assessment of your parish, notice if there are any areas that may require more work. If there are, the work can often be done through delegation, which was addressed in chapter 3.

Summary: The Sacred Ground of the Other

"The place on which you are standing is holy ground." (Exod. 3:5)

The world is rapidly changing. Conventional models of formation may not be sufficient or efficient for spreading the gospel to younger generations. It is crucial that a catechetical leader take all factors that may affect the ministry into consideration and adapt to them to serve the needs of people. These challenges should not hinder or prohibit us from creating new ways to convey the teachings of the Lord to a very mobile society. Rather, we are called to embrace the sacred ground of the other.

For Reflection and Discussion

- What new understanding or inspiration do you have now that you didn't have before?
- Does your catechetical program respond to the needs of different ethnic groups in your parish? Does it address common issues in the lives of adults?

Growing as a Catechetical Leader

It is essential to know the terrain before you begin planning for faith formation. New societal factors are shaping behaviors and practices: blended families, digital technologies, fewer faith-formation processes, and cross-cultural populations. These are challenges that the traditional model of faith formation does not address. List factors that shape the present realities of your parish (ethnicities, types of families, digital technologies, and so on).

Go to www.loyolapress.com/ECL to access the worksheet.

Suggested Action

Do not be afraid to engage grandparents in the faith lives of their grandchildren. They are jewels of wisdom and are usually willing to share their faith with younger people.

For Further Consideration

The Catechetical Leader in the Third Millennium. New York State Catholic Conference (September 26, 2012), www.nyscatholic.org/2012/09/2001/.

Amoris Laetitia. (The Joy of Love). Pope Francis (Frederick, MD: The Word Among Us, 2016).

National Study of Youth and Religion. (Research project directed by Christian Smith, University of Notre Dame, and Lisa Pearce, University of North Carolina at Chapel Hill), http://youthandreligion.nd.edu/.

8

Make Up Your Mind: Leadership and Decision Making

The Dark Knight

In the Batman movie *The Dark Knight*, there are two instances where decisions need to be made. In one scene, the Joker reveals that Rachel and Dent have been trapped in separate locations rigged with explosives. Batman must decide to save the woman he loves, Rachel, or the man who can help save the city, Dent. Batman decides to save the love of his life; unfortunately, the Joker tricks Batman by switching the locations, and when Batman goes for Rachel he ends up going to Dent's location instead. Both places explode, leaving Dent with half a face and killing Rachel. In the second instance, the Joker has filled two ferries with explosives; these ferries are evacuating people to safety. One carries civilians and the other carries prison inmates. Devices on each ferry make it possible for its passengers to blow up the other ferry. If, by a certain time, one of the ferries has not been blown up, the Joker will destroy both ferries. Both groups refuse to blow the other up, but time is running out. What is Batman to do? Should he help the civilians' boat only? Or should he try to mediate between both groups? Or should he try to catch the Joker and eliminate these tragic possible outcomes?

Both scenes demonstrate the complexity and difficulty of decision making. Decisions are part of daily life, but it is sometimes difficult to make sound, effective decisions. Often we are not choosing between obvious good and bad outcomes but between two good ones. The question is, which is better for this situation? Such discernment is a big part of your responsibility as a catechetical leader.

Just Do It?

Although some life decisions can be as drastic and life-threatening as the examples I gave from the movie *The Dark Knight*, the good thing is that as a catechetical leader, you will most likely not find yourself in such dire situations. Instead, you will or may already be confronted with pastoral dilemmas that need answers or directions that bring people closer to Christ. Perhaps you have already experienced people looking for simple answers, as though everything were black and white. You, on the other hand, recognize that there is always a certain amount of gray area in life. It is your role to make the best possible decisions and to help others practice the art of sound decision making, too.

Making Decisions with Integrity

Because of your leadership position, a variety of people—including catechists, parents, and fellow staff members—will seek you out for guidance and direction. It is in the nature of your position that people will come to you with their brokenness, looking for healing, reassurance, or affirmation. Not every decision you make can "fix" things, and it is important to recognize that there will be times when people seek you out for spiritual counseling that may be beyond your capacity. It's very important that you refer them to the right people, such as your pastor or someone with professional counseling skills.

Certain issues require other people to be involved in your decisions. For instance, if you're changing times and dates for your catechetical program, it would be good to consult with parents, catechists, and other pastoral staff to discuss how this change might impact your parish as a whole. Other decisions, such as selecting a theme for a prayer service, will not require consultation. Some decisions will be easy to make, and others will require that you gather information, identify alternatives, and discern options before taking action.

Restless Hearts

Our human condition gives us competing desires: to have control over our own lives on the one hand and to cultivate a spiritual life and follow the will of God on the other. It is a constant struggle for us to let go of our egos and allow God's Spirit to dwell in our lives. It can sometimes feel like a divided heart: following our own needs and wants versus sacrificing them for the good of others. What a dilemma! We may find ourselves asking, "What does God want of me? What does my entire being want?" Saint Augustine famously prayed, "Lord, give me chastity and continency, only not yet." He also concluded, however, that "our hearts are restless till they find rest in you." Our decisions, if they follow the will of God, will ultimately bring rest to our restless hearts.

How to Make Good Choices

In the book *What's Your Decision?* Sparough, Manney, and Hipskind propose that any decision one makes surely matters to God. They recount the story of Saint Ignatius of Loyola walking the road and discussing religion with a non-Christian man shortly after Ignatius's own conversion. The discussion grew heated, and, where the road divided, the non-Christian man abruptly departed, hurling an insult about the Blessed Virgin Mary. Still thinking like a military man, Ignatius's first impulse was to go after the man and defend the honor of Mary by killing him. His newfound faith, however, urged him to take the other path and let it go. Not yet grasping the full complexity of discernment, Ignatius decided to leave it to his donkey to make the decision. If the donkey took the road the other man had taken, Ignatius would pursue him and kill him, but if the donkey chose the other road, Ignatius would let go of his anger and go away peacefully. Thankfully for Ignatius and for all of us, the donkey took the peaceful road (11). This experience led Ignatius to delve more deeply into the concept of discernment: to consider his motives and why he had reacted the way he did. He realized that his emotions were connected to his reactions, and later to his decisions, but that emotions alone cannot always be trusted.

Yes, our emotions should play an important role in any discernment process. They can give us important information about what we value and where our investments lie. But we need to balance our emotions—what we feel like doing—with God's will for us, which is to do the loving thing. We must also use our capacity to reason, or think through, our options logically. Saint Ignatius of Loyola knew what it meant to be torn between the two human impulses of logical reasoning and emotional reaction, but he also learned over time that God speaks to us through our human nature. We have been wired to hear God through "our emotional responses to the experiences we have" (ibid., 33) and then to reflect upon what we hear. The goal of discernment isn't to just do what feels right but to use our emotions and our reason to make decisions that help us follow God.

The Discernment Process

During the process of making decisions, spiritual discernment should not be seen as one small step along the way. Rather, discernment should be seen and understood primarily as a spiritual movement through which we allow the Holy Spirit to give direction on a matter that holds the potential to draw us closer to God. Spiritual discernment is more than a skill; it is a gift from God. My colleague and friend Joe Paprocki describes discernment as the interior process "to align our will with the will of God so that we can learn what God is calling us to do and become" (*7 Keys to Spiritual Wellness*, 36). So, how do we align our will with God's will? The key is to love God first, as Ignatius believed, so that God, in turn, will direct us to our deepest desires and invite us to shape our will to his.

Obviously, as catechetical leaders we cannot make decisions solely on personal presumptions or preferences—which would be to act as rulers or dictators. Instead, we need to remind ourselves that we have been called to be disciples of Jesus Christ and to act in his name. As the *General Directory for Catechesis* states, "Faith is a personal encounter with Jesus Christ making of oneself a disciple of him. This demands a permanent commitment to think like him, to judge like him and to live as he lived" (#53). This implies that as catechetical leaders we are called to learn to entrust our actions and their outcomes to God, to rely on him, and to continue to engage in the dynamic movement of the Spirit.

Discerning the Holy Spirit when making decisions should not be divorced from your dreams, images, feelings, logical reasoning, and intuition. Rather, God uses all of these vehicles to communicate the best possible route available to us when faced with a decision. It is no surprise that in July 2016, Pope Francis invited the Jesuits to begin an outreach to diocesan priests to teach them the art of discernment as taught by Saint Ignatius of Loyola. Ignatian spirituality offers a pathway for making complex decisions in the face of conflict, and this approach can and should play a significant role in your work as a catechetical leader. For Ignatius, knowing what was moral and immoral was essential, but even more important was knowing the movement of the Spirit in the life of the person. Here are some of Ignatius's principles of discernment.

- **Decision making is a struggle, and we should embrace it.**
  Ignatius believed the battle is the problem itself but also the
  process of finding a solution to the problem.
- **Feelings have spiritual meaning.** Ignatius experienced opposite
  emotions, but he was able to distinguish subtle movements
  whereby God communicated his will.
- **God is always a loving God.** Ignatius believed that the end in
  every situation is always God, and our decisions should be means
  to help us reach that end.
- **The Spirit longs to guide our discernment process.** To
  determine the extent to which we are involving the Spirit in our
  discernment process, we can ask:

  ○ Does my decision lead me and others closer to Christ?
  ○ Does my decision inspire me to love?
  ○ Does my decision give me freedom of spirit? What emotions
    might be stirring in my body (peace or a lack thereof, joy,
    anxiety, love)?

In practical terms, discernment should involve the following steps:

1. **Identify the dilemma.** Take some time to precisely identify the
   nature of the problem. For example, is the problem rooted in
   conflicting or unproductive attitudes, a lack of understanding,
   competition, or something else?
2. **Gather data.** Gather the most important information needed.
   What key facts do I have or need to obtain?
3. **Start with what you know.** Get to know your information. How
   did this happen? What led to this? What is the magnitude of the
   problem? Who else is involved? You may want to share the
   information with a group of people. Remember, you don't have

to have all the answers. Never underestimate the wisdom found in a group!

4. **Identify alternatives.** Ask yourself what other options are available. How many options are there?

5. **Make a list of pros and cons.** Write out a list of the pros and cons that you can identify.

6. **Ask for guidance.** Take all you know into prayer. Ask the Holy Spirit to guide you and to lead you to God's will.

7. **Let God speak to you.** Listen to your emotions and thoughts. What do you hear? What keeps running through your mind?

8. **Choose among your options.** Slowly review all the information you have. Are there any inconsistencies? What's the worst that could happen? What's the best that could happen? If needed, talk it over once again with a confidant.

9. **Make a decision and take action.** After doing so, evaluate the fruits of your actions. Are there any parts of the decision that need to be reevaluated? Was this an effective decision? Was anything learned? Did the decision lead people closer to God's will?

Decision-Making Styles

Not everyone has the same decision-making style. According to Brent Gleeson in *Forbes* magazine, November 7, 2012, there are four basic decision-making styles:

1. Command—A leader makes decisions without consulting his or her team.

2. Collaborative—A leader gathers the team and requests feedback and insights in order to make a more informed decision.

3. Consensus—A leader bases decisions on the willingness of all involved to abide by it, even if not everyone fully agrees with it.

4. Convenience—A leader delegates a decision by empowering trusted peers. ("4 Ways for Leaders to Make a Decision," November 7, 2012)

You may find yourself employing one or more of these styles, depending on the nature of the decision at hand. Not every decision requires the consensus of a large group of people; that would be neither realistic nor efficient.

Some decisions, of course, do require a great amount of collaboration and consensus. A few years ago, at a suburban Houston parish, the pastor decided to make changes to the operational hours and services of the parish without consulting parishioners, staff, or the pastoral council. He decided that receptionist hours needed to be extended from 9:00 a.m. to 7:00 p.m. to serve the needs of people coming to the parish right after work, and he expected pastoral staff only and not administrative staff to work around this schedule. He also changed the time for one Sunday Mass from 10:30 a.m. to 9:00 a.m. because there was too much of a gap between the 7:00 a.m. Mass and 10:30 a.m. Mass. Unfortunately, the pastor didn't realize the impact this change would have on the faith-formation program, since children attended class from 9:00 a.m. to 10:25 a.m., after which the entire family attended Mass together. Now there was no way of participating together during this time—unless, of course, the catechetical program changed its hours to accommodate the pastor's wishes.

At first, the pastor was reluctant to reverse his decisions because he believed that they were good for the entire community. Eventually, however, after a large number of complaints from the entire parish, the pastor relinquished his decision and went back to previous hours of operation. What went wrong? He is the pastor and has the right to make decisions, doesn't he? Well, yes and no. While he has the authority to make such decisions, it was clearly not wise to do so unilaterally when so many people would be affected.

As a catechetical leader, be sure to take all participating parties into consideration before making a decision. Here are just a few examples of the types of decisions you may face as a catechetical leader, often in conjunction with your pastor and pastoral staff.

- Which textbook series and resources you will use
- What format your faith-formation program will follow
- Who will teach which level and/or program
- On what day(s) and time(s) your faith-formation program(s) will take place
- Whether a catechist should be kept or dismissed
- Whether a child needs disciplinary action for unacceptable behavior
- Whether an individual is fully prepared or predisposed to receive a sacrament
- How to allocate funds in your budget
- How much time, energy, and money you can spend on your own ongoing formation
- What information should go toward your program's newsletter, Facebook page, Twitter account, or Web site
- Whether to allow a field trip
- Whom to recruit as catechist aides
- How to structure catechist formation
- When and on what issues the pastor needs to be consulted
- How best to arrange your own schedule (which meetings/gatherings to attend, when to take vacation time, etc.)
- Which duties and responsibilities to delegate, and to whom
- What to say or how to offer help to a struggling catechist

Don't Be Afraid to Make Mistakes

Leadership in a parish setting has some similarities to leadership in the corporate world; however, success for a parish catechetical leader is measured by drawing people to Christ, not increasing the bottom line. Effective catechetical leadership is not a one-person show. We rely on the wisdom, intelligence, and resourcefulness of others.

There are no crystal balls telling us what direction to take in life or what lies in the future. But we do have plenty of resources at our disposal, including our conscience, our ability to act, our emotions, our reason, our instincts, and the wisdom of our community and tradition. In the process of making a decision, it is important to consider all of these sources of information, as well as to distinguish between our own desires and God's. If your ultimate desire is to love God and respond to his call, keeping this in mind will make decisions much easier—and your decisions are much more likely to be configured to God's will. Do not be afraid to make mistakes; the saints made them too. As you give more and more of yourself to the service of your ministry, the Lord will guide you to serve and lead others in ever more profound ways.

Summary: I Have Set before You Life and Death

"I call heaven and earth to witness against you today that I have set before you life and death, blessings and curses. Choose life so that you and your descendants may live, loving the Lord your God." (Deut. 30:19–20)

It is inevitable that as a catechetical leader, you will be faced with many different decisions. Some will be simple, minimal decisions that do not affect large numbers of people; others will be complex decisions that affect many people in significant ways. Catechetical leaders have the responsibility to make the best possible decisions for everyone involved and should therefore consciously adopt and use a decision-making process or structure. God has given you the capacity to choose good over evil, and you should take this capacity seriously. As we know, life is messy and complex, and there will be times when it is difficult to know whether you are making the right decision. As a ministry grows, needed decisions become more frequent, complicated, and consequential. The key is to seek the guidance of the Holy Spirit.

For Reflection and Discussion

- What has been the most difficult decision you have made in your role as catechetical leader?
- What style of decision making do you most often adopt?

Growing as a Catechetical Leader

Making decisions is a lifelong process that requires being attuned to your emotions, gathering information, and thinking clearly and logically. Some people find this process to be tedious and prefer quick, black-and-white answers. They may come to you because you have the positional power to make decisions. Do not be pressured into hasty decisions, however. Follow the steps of discernment outlined in this chapter, and feel free to adjust and adapt them depending on the issue being discerned.

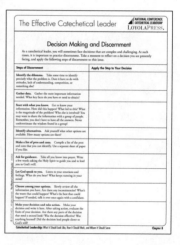

Go to www.loyolapress.com/ECL to access the worksheet.

Suggested Action

Do not be afraid to make mistakes along the way. Saint Ignatius (and almost every other saint) had to learn how to discern God's will in his decision-making process. You don't have to make perfect decisions every time, but do try to avoid making impromptu decisions without discerning the impact they will have on others.

For Further Consideration

What's Your Decision?: How to Make Choices with Confidence and Clarity. Michael Sparough, SJ, Jim Manney, and Tim Hipskind, SJ (Chicago: Loyola Press, 2010).

Discovering Your Dream: How Ignatian Spirituality Can Guide Your Life. Gerald M. Fagin, SJ (Chicago: Loyola Press, 2013).

God's Voice Within: The Ignatian Way to Discover God's Will. Mark Thibodeaux (Chicago: Loyola Press, 2010).

Discernment: The Art of Choosing Well. Pierre Wolff (Liguori, MO: Liguori Publications, 2012).

9

Smoothing Out the Rough Spots: Leadership and Conflict

Firework

Several years ago I hosted a meeting at my parish in which things didn't quite go the way I had planned. I felt frustrated, powerless, and bitter. I felt as if all my planning had gone down the drain. Even though I had tried many ways of bringing this group together, I was having no success. Weeks went by, and my frustration was so evident that people could see it in my face. Thinking about the "stubborn people" on that team made me not want to attend the next meeting. I just didn't want to address the issues at hand because I didn't know how. The easier thing to do was to blame other people for manipulating the agenda.

One evening, as I was driving home, my six-year-old daughter was riding in the back seat and singing a song by Taylor Swift called "Shake It Off." As I paid attention to what she was singing, the tune easily got into my head, and I found myself breathing a sigh of relief. I felt as if the weight of the world had been lifted from my shoulders. As we arrived at home, I was again reassured when the next song started to play: "Firework," by Katy Perry, which sings of holding on to a spark of hope in the face of despair.

That music, at that moment, was God's divine providence. It gave me the energy and the tranquility I needed to deal with the difficult issue at work. With better focus and perspective, I was able to concentrate on what had actually gone wrong at the meeting and whom I needed to talk to in order to resolve the conflict. My stress levels went down, I felt calm and secure, and I had control of my emotions. When the next meeting came, I was prepared to resolve the situation. A spiritual transformation happened in that room—not just for me but for the entire group. We had all been seeking healing but had been unable to voice our frustration and hurt until now.

Wisdom

Most of us know the biblical story of how King Solomon listened to a dispute between two women claiming to be the mother of a baby and how Solomon was unable to determine who was speaking the truth. After listening to the women and giving the matter much thought, he called for his swordsman and ordered him to cut the child's body into two pieces and give each woman one half. The real mother screamed in horror at the thought of having her beloved child die and pleaded with Solomon to give the child to the other woman. Solomon knew at once who the mother of the baby was (1 Kings 3:16–28). Because of this and other decisions Solomon made, he was considered the wisest of the kings of Israel.

Unfortunately, wisdom can sometimes be a rare commodity in leadership. A common mistake many leaders make when trying to resolve conflicts is to believe that their opinion is the only correct one. This attitude that "I have it right all the time" will not serve you well in the ministry of catechetical leadership. Rather, as Tom Rath and Barry Conchie emphasize in their book *Strengths Based Leadership* (Gallup Press, 2008), effective leadership, especially in pastoral ministry, is about leading people with harmony by seeking areas of agreement (175). When tensions mount, your role as a catechetical leader is to utilize your skills to reduce friction and find common ground among all parties. This requires the art of listening, the gift of creativity, and the ability to honor everyone's views and opinions.

Peace of Mind

Most of us would like to live a life without conflict. In fact, we are sometimes surprised when a conflict arises, especially in a ministerial setting, where charity and love are supposed to prevail. Nevertheless, conflict, like decision making, is a part of any relationship, whether it be at home, in a parish, or in one's social life. Conflict is inevitable. No relationship is immune to conflict. And yet when there is conflict between two individuals or among the members of a group, those involved often get angry, offended, embittered, or defensive. Sometimes conflict leads to the end of a relationship or to ongoing resentment. It is the job of an effective leader not to avoid conflict but to take action and respond to the needs and interests of those involved. Leadership is not something you can put on and take off as needed. You are a leader 24/7, and occasionally you will be tested with conflicts.

Conflict can have constructive or destructive results. It all depends on whether you as a catechetical leader can find a way to make moments of conflict sacred and uplifting—even though consensus may not be reached. To resolve conflicts constructively, the parties involved must be clear about what the problems are and concentrate on what each person needs in order to feel a sense of resolution. Positive results can be achieved if you, as a catechetical leader, do your homework before trying to resolve the conflict. What is involved in this homework? Consider the following:

1. An effective leader recognizes or anticipates conflict and asks . . .

   • What are my own interests?
   • What are my concerns, hopes, and fears?

- Is this conflict coming to light because of some other unresolved conflict?
- Are we dealing with superficial conflict or a systemic problem?

2. An effective leader understands the conflict's potential for creativity and asks . . .

- What are the needs of all parties involved?
- What are their concerns, hopes, and fears?

3. An effective catechetical leader gives proper attention to different possible outcomes and asks . . .

- What kinds of agreements might we reach?

Conflict can be managed in a positive way when the leader clarifies expectations and roles, seeks to understand both sides of the conflict, strengthens relationships, and creates opportunities for innovation. Yes, these things can be hard to do—just like many other parts of your job as a catechetical leader, such as avoiding favoritism, discrimination, and prejudice; maintaining professional balance; and reaching decisions without compromise. Fortunately, when the task of conflict resolution arises, there are some concrete things you can do to minimize the difficulty.

Mistakes to Avoid

While some conflicts arise from personality differences, others come from disagreements about the nature of the ministry and how it is being accomplished. In groups where people often express different opinions, the process of working through conflict can take longer and can be painful for individuals whose ideas are rejected. Individuals in conflict often get stuck on the problems and have difficulty looking at solutions. How can you, as a team leader, help those in conflict move from problem to solution? From my own experience of dealing with conflicts in ministry, here are some principles I recommend.

- **Do not ignore the conflict.** Conflicts can fester when ignored.
- **Avoid communicating via e-mail.** This leaves too much room for misinterpretation. It's always better to talk in person.
- **Invite all parties to voice their views.** Some people just don't say anything until they are ready to explode. Pay attention to introverts, and invite them to express themselves.
- **Avoid making assumptions.** Talk directly to each party in order to understand the issue more fully.
- **Show respect for all parties involved.** When people don't feel valued or don't feel as if they are being heard, they are resistant to any resolution.
- **Avoid a combat mentality.** Strive not to be defensive, and avoid thinking that there must be a winner and a loser. Think win-win.
- **Do not overgeneralize or blame someone.** Keep the issues impersonal and be objective.
- **Deal with the conflict, not the person.** Good people can disagree; avoid vilifying people who disagree with you.
- **Avoid taking things personally.** Separate your personal feelings from the issues that need to be resolved.

Focus on the Solution

In her book *Redeeming Conflict* (Ave Maria Press, 2016), Ann Garrido explains that when conflicts do occur and someone gets hurt, the challenge for the victim is to have the courage "to go talk directly to the person who has hurt or angered you" (16). This is not easy, but taking the first step is necessary. In the Gospel of Matthew, Jesus teaches his disciples that when conflicts and confrontations occur, the Christian way of handling them is to talk to the offender.

> If another member of the church sins against you, go and point out the fault when the two of you are alone. If the member listens to you, you have regained that one. But if you are not listened to, take one or two others along with you, so that every word may be confirmed by the evidence of two or three witnesses. (Matt. 18:15–16)

Let's face it—not everyone can be expected to agree on everything at all times. Learning to agree to disagree can be a healthy step in establishing mutual respect without offending another party. I have found that most conflicts can eventually be resolved with the proper approach—which sometimes includes patience. It is important that as a catechetical leader you allow others to express their disagreements and assure them that resolution is possible, even if not immediately.

Garrido also explains that in some instances, either the offender or the offended runs into the temptation of avoiding uncomfortable conversations and instead turns to passive-aggressive behavior or seeks to exert influence by using a method called triangulation. This method occurs when one of the conflicted parties forms an alliance with a third person and then brings that person in to mediate in his or her favor—to serve as a "rescuer." This mode of operation violates human dignity and violates the principle of subsidiarity—granting power to the lowest or smallest levels of an organization—because other people are brought into the conflict without allowing it to be managed by the particular individuals involved (*Redeeming Conflict*, 15).

Those individuals may avoid conflict because they mistakenly believe that dealing directly with the offender or the offended can be seen only as confrontation. However, as a pastoral minister, your goal is always reconciliation. Following are a few more steps you can take to bring people in conflict together:

1. When involved in a conflict, pause to get your own emotions in check. Pause, count to ten, and take a deep breath.

2. Open yourself to hear and listen to the other person. Predispose yourself to accept a time and a place to discuss the conflict.

3. If you are completely out of touch with your emotions or feel so stressed that you can pay attention to only a limited number of feelings, you may have a hard time communicating effectively with the other person. Try to stay calm, manage your stress, control your emotions, and don't let frustration or anger dominate you.

4. Speak clearly and state the problem as you see it by making "I" statements. Avoid making any judgments or absolute statements using *never* or *always*. Instead, use statements such as "I want to understand or know what you are really hoping for."

5. Listen to the other person, and do not interrupt. You may feel tempted to intervene and contradict what the other person is saying, but doing so will only escalate the tension and make resolution more difficult. Notice what is being communicated both verbally and nonverbally. Be willing to forgive. Let go of the urge to punish or make someone feel bad.

6. Seek to de-escalate the situation, avoiding words that you will only regret later. Consider using humor if appropriate.

7. Ask questions and seek clarification. Use statements such as "Can you say more about that?" and "Where did this happen?" *Who, what, where,* and *when* questions are all acceptable. Avoid asking *why* questions because they can sound accusatory.

8. Avoid using words like *ought* or *should*. Ask open-ended questions such as "How can we resolve this?" Restate what you have heard and be concise.

9. Stick to one conflict at a time; do not change the subject until the concern has been addressed. Seek to establish common ground. What do you and the other party have in common? Do you agree on something? It's better to focus on points of

agreement than on points of disagreement. Validate the concerns of the other person. Build "power with," not "power over."

10. Brainstorm several solutions, always working toward a win-win. Make a list of possible ways to remove obstacles from the path of harmony. Ask for help or invite another perspective from an objective party. (To avoid triangulation, make sure the party is truly objective.)

11. Choose the best resolution. You cannot change others' behaviors, but you can prevent certain behaviors from reappearing. Offer options that both parties seem to agree with. Suggest a timetable for implementing a way to resolve the conflict.

12. Thank the person(s) for listening. If the discussion breaks down, schedule another time to meet and, if possible, consider bringing someone else to mediate.

13. Finally, while you may want to avoid anger, do not fear it. Anger, in some cases, is an appropriate emotion—we call it "righteous anger," the kind of anger God expresses in Scripture when his people reject his love and mercy. Just be sure that your anger is indeed "righteous" and that its purpose is not to attack or tear down another.

Checkmate Is Not the Goal

During my teenage years, the song "Difícil" ("Difficult") by the Mexican rock band El TRI was constantly played on the radio. The song speaks about how everything in life is complicated and similar to a chess game: everyone wants to checkmate the king and achieve total victory. In reality, however, there will always be tensions pulling you in different directions. Each of these tensions could potentially lead to conflict, and so you have to "choose your battles wisely." The goal is to keep yourself focused on building the kingdom of God, creating a sense of community, and continuing to sustain the mission of the Church.

In his book *7 Habits of Highly Effective People* (Free Press, 2004), author Stephen Covey points out that the most effective leaders seek a win-win solution to conflicts. The goal is not the destruction and defeat of the other person but the mutual benefit of all parties involved. The solution is not "my way or the highway" but rather the creation of an "our way" of resolving the conflict. In order to achieve a win-win solution, you will need to be able to see things from the other person's point of view—not as a chess game in which you must dominate.

Jesus Faced Conflict

Sometimes making the tough call can lead to conflict or disagreements. Don't feel discouraged. Jesus dealt with conflict constantly. He encountered disagreements with others about God's law, the Sabbath, traditions, and his own authority. Take a look at the Scripture passages below, and reflect on what you can learn from how Jesus handled disagreements.

- Luke 9:46 (tempering ambition with humility)
- Luke 12:58 (settling with an opponent)
- Matt. 15:3–9 (conflict with the scribes and Pharisees)
- Matt. 12:9–14 (healing on the Sabbath)
- John 4:7–10 (the Samaritan woman)

Summary: From Conflict to Harmony

A soft answer turns away wrath,
but a harsh word stirs up anger. (Prov. 15:1)

Resolving conflict in a positive manner can lead to much-improved professional and personal relationships. It is important to be able to identify conflict in the workplace and know how to act quickly and effectively. Whether you are dealing with a disagreement between coworkers or among a group of volunteers, if done well, conflict resolution can save relationships and resources while improving the life of the parish community. In fact, it has been proven that most successful leaders are not those who always agree with their followers but instead those who have developed strong teams that focus on results rather than on conflicts (Tom Rath and Barry Conchie, *Strengths Based Leadership*, 71). Such teams are capable of converting trials that could lead to breakdown into opportunities to grow stronger and more cohesive—and they do this by staying focused on the mission. In our case, continuing the mission of the church and building the Body of Christ should be our focus.

For Reflection and Discussion

- Recall a conflict you recently had. What approach did you take to resolve it? What could you have done differently?
- List three significant situations in which you experienced conflict that had an effect on your ministry.

Growing as a Catechetical Leader

We all experience conflict. Some experience it more often than others by virtue of their leadership position. Nevertheless, working on conflict resolution is an indication of maturity, integrity, and character that can bring the best out of you. Learning to agree to disagree is part of the growing process. If you find yourself in a dilemma, don't be afraid to use the tools offered in this chapter.

Go to www.loyolapress.com/ECL to access the worksheet.

Suggested Action

Remember, approaching and talking to someone with whom you have a conflict does not equal—but is an attempt to achieve—reconciliation. In the days ahead, identify someone with whom you are experiencing a conflict. Pray for this person and then approach him or her with an invitation to resolve the matter.

For Further Consideration

Redeeming Conflict: 12 Habits for Christian Leaders. Ann M. Garrido (Notre Dame, IN: Ave Maria Press, 2016).

Strengths Based Leadership. Tom Rath and Barry Conchie (New York: Gallup Press, 2008).

"Managing Conflict in the Church," H. Jack Morris, *Ministry*, May 2001, www.ministrymagazine.org/archive/2001/05/ managing-conflict-in-the-church.html.

When Ministry Is Messy. Richard C. Brown (Cincinnati, OH: Franciscan Media, 2006).

The Leadership Book. Charles J. Keating (Mahwah, NJ: Paulist Press, 1977).

10

Unabashedly Catholic: Leadership and Robust Catholic Identity

New Frontiers

Some time ago I was in conversation with my maternal grandfather to wish him a happy birthday. He shared how grateful he was to God for the many blessings he had seen throughout his life. Somehow, we ended up talking about his parents, uncles, and aunts, and how large an extended family he had all over the U.S. and France. As my grandfather was sharing the stories, I got to thinking about the possibility of creating a family tree. I tried to do so on my own but couldn't go further back than two generations. I had no idea it was going to be so difficult. During the process of research, I began with the easiest part—me.

I was born in El Paso, Texas, but most of my early life was spent in Ciudad Juárez, which lies just south of El Paso on the other side of the Rio Grande. The interesting thing, as I recall, was that the English language and American cultural values that are dear to El Pasoans were only a secondary influence in my life and were not a part of my core identity. It took several years for me to be fully immersed in both cultures and to adapt to different lifestyles. For instance, I was taught to memorize the Mexican National Anthem and to salute the Mexican flag at school. I learned the cultural customs, values, TV shows, practices, traditions, and history of Mexico. I was born in the Catholic faith, and (as it was in El Paso) the Catholic faith in Ciudad Juárez was central to daily life.

The challenge for me came during the high school years. I was already attending high school on the west side of El Paso and once was invited to a football game by one of my friends. We got to the stadium, and before the game began everyone was invited to sing the national anthem. I stood up but felt embarrassed because I didn't know the words to the song, so I just mimicked the people around me who were singing with so much passion. My friend obviously noticed, but he didn't say anything until after the game. He understood because he knew I wasn't the only Chicano person (a Mexican-American living in the United States) in El Paso! This episode triggered in me a desire to solidify my identity as a U.S. Hispanic Catholic. I wanted to do this not so much to blend in with society but to know my true calling and identity. Our identity grounds us, centers us, and guides our thoughts and actions. When we lose that center, we can easily lose ourselves, especially in the face of uncertainty.

Identity Card

One of the greatest challenges the U.S. Catholic Church faces today is the growing trend toward the lack of a vibrant Catholic identity. Study after study reveals that young people actively practice religion less and find it less significant or relevant to their lives than previous generations did, even as they sometimes continue to identify with the external symbols of Catholicism.

As a catechetical leader, you are called to a form of leadership that reflects and transmits the core values, beliefs, and practices of Catholicism. Just as our physical identity can be established by fingerprints and dental records, the spiritual identity we receive in baptism is permanent and cannot be taken away. As catechetical leaders, we need to continually strive to help people embrace their Catholic identity in the twenty-first century.

Living up to the Family Name

Anyone who comes from a large family, as I do, knows that each sibling feels pressure to live up to the family name. Parents often remind children of what their name "represents" and how their name suggests a standard of behavior. Families develop what can be thought of as a "way of proceeding"—a modus operandi (M.O.), so to speak. The Society of Jesus (the Jesuits) use this phrase—a *way of proceeding*—to refer to the "attitudes, values, and patterns of behavior" (*General Congregation* 34, Decree 26), drawn from the life and person of Saint Ignatius of Loyola, that guide the society's work.

In a similar way, all Catholics have a way of proceeding—a set of "attitudes, values, and patterns of behavior," drawn from the life and teachings of Jesus Christ, Mary, and the saints, that guides everything we do. As a catechetical leader, you are called not only to follow this way of proceeding but to invite and teach others to do the same. In other words, if your leadership style were to be analyzed, what should be most evident is a Catholic M.O.

Bearing a Resemblance to God

Around the time Pope Saint John XXIII convened the Second Vatican Council (1962–1965), Cardinal Donald Wuerl was a young priest. He recalls that, as the Church sought to implement the profound vision of this Council, there were also "experimentation and confusion" that sometimes led people in the Church to reduce their understanding of faith to "vaguely positive feelings about God" (Cardinal Donald Wuerl, *Being Catholic Today*, 16). The Church was not alone in its experience of tumult. The 1960s saw extraordinary events such as the rise of The Beatles; the assassinations of President John F. Kennedy, his brother Bobby Kennedy, and Dr. Martin Luther King Jr.; the civil rights movement; the Vietnam War; and the first moon landing. All these events, both positive and negative, resulted in people questioning long-standing norms and values.

Catholic identity, however, is rooted in the unchanging reality of our Creator. As Pope Francis noted, "Our 'identity card' is found in the fact that mankind was created 'in the image, in the likeness of God.'" He asks the fundamental questions, "How can I know the image of God? How can I know what He is like to know what I'm like?" He then responds by saying that the only way of knowing our true identity card is to "take up the journey . . . [and] get to know the face of God" (*L'Osservatore Romano*, February 13, 2015). In other words, if we really want to know our true identity as Catholics, we have to know our Creator and the purpose for which we were created.

The *Catechism of the Catholic Church* explains that "the desire for God is written in the human heart" and that "God never ceases to draw man to himself. Only in God will [man] find the truth and happiness he never stops searching for" (#27). At the core of our humanity, there is always this thirst for true meaning and purpose in life. This is actually the journey of life. The heart of the human was made to be restless unless it rests in God, to paraphrase Saint Augustine. Just as in the story of the two disciples on the road to Emmaus, we sometimes are unable to recognize Christ—the answer to our restlessness—even as our hearts burn for him.

This flame that burns in our hearts and incites us to follow God can be attributed to the graces received by the virtue of baptism. We Christians were given a new identity and made into a new creation on the day we were baptized, making us new in Christ "as a new creature" (*CCC,* #1214). Because of this gift, pastoral ministers cannot simply be bystanders or "seated Christians," as Pope Francis calls it

(*L'Osservatore Romano*, February 13, 2015). By the gift of baptism, all Christians have a role and identity to play in the life and mission of the church. It is for this reason that there can't be "partial Catholics" who separate faith from daily living.

In his apostolic exhortation *Evangelii Gaudium,* Pope Francis affirms that because of baptism, everyone shares in the responsibility of carrying out the mission of the church to evangelize and draw people into intimate communion with Christ:

> In virtue of their baptism, all the members of the People of God have become missionary disciples. . . . All the baptized, whatever their position in the Church or their level of instruction in the faith, are agents of evangelization. . . . Every Christian is challenged, here and now, to be actively engaged. (#120)

This is not simply the work of the clergy but of all those baptized into Christ. It is the responsibility of catechetical leaders to help motivate, inspire, and awaken in people's hearts a desire to follow Christ. On more than one occasion I have personally heard Cardinal Daniel DiNardo of Galveston-Houston tell people that following Christ requires work, which means there is no one unemployed within the Body of Christ. Every one of us has a responsibility and a duty to build the kingdom of God here on earth and to continue to further the mission of the Church by spreading the gospel through our deeds and words, as directed by our Lord Jesus Christ.

Plan of Holiness

To be Catholic is to believe, proclaim, model, live, and celebrate the passion, death, and resurrection of Jesus Christ. Christians are called to be configured to and to imitate Christ. As Pope Benedict XVI explained, "The Church's deepest nature is expressed in her three-fold responsibility: of proclaiming the word of God (*kerygma-martyria*), celebrating the sacraments (*leitourgia*), and exercising the ministry of charity (*diakonia*)" (*Deus Caritas Est*, #25). This is our Catholic M.O.—our way of proceeding.

Let's take a look at these three basic actions that lie at the core of our Catholic identity.

Witness (*Kerygma/Martyria*)

Catholic identity is shaped by these fundamental actions: how I live and how I witness about my faith to others. Do I really walk the walk and talk the talk? Do my words match my actions? Owen Phelps writes that when people know someone is a Christian and see that person fail miserably in living up to the faith's standards and ideals, it surely will impact Christianity. As a result, some choose not to give public witness to their Catholic faith, thinking that "at least we can't be accused of giving Christianity a bad name" (*The Catholic Vision for Leading Like Jesus* [Huntington, IN: Our Sunday Visitor, 2014], 30). The responsibility to give witness to our faith begins with us as catechetical leaders. People need to see us boldly and joyfully practice what we preach.

Catholic witness entails much more than simply spouting doctrinal concepts. While it is about words, it is also about actions and personal testimony that can either inspire others to search for holiness or hinder them. Cardinal Wuerl explains that during the second century, a notable voice in Christianity, Tertullian, described how Christians bore the mark of their master—love—through their actions. Christians helped others even at the risk of losing their lives. According to Tertullian, "Christians 'supply the wants of destitute orphans, and of old persons who are homebound; those who have suffered shipwreck, or have been condemned to the mines, or banished to the islands, or shut up in prisons'" (*Being Catholic Today*, 10).

Blessed Pope Paul VI wrote that "modern man listens more willingly to witnesses than to teachers, and if he does listen to teachers it is because they are witnesses" (*Evangelii Nuntiandi*, 41). Who are the influential leaders for today's generation? Who are the Catholic leaders who, through witness, can inspire younger generations? It is no surprise that Saint Mother Teresa of Calcutta drew attention, not because of her image or reputation or because of what others saw in her but because of her simplicity, her life of prayer, and her integrity. This way of proceeding influenced younger generations—especially women—to adopt this type of lifestyle.

People today are too often taught to worry about their reputation or image rather than their core identity or conscience. Certain virtues like humility, justice, and courage build character. And through character, Catholic identity is strengthened. "Character is based on the integrity of the leader as a human being," writes Dan Ebener, "whereas reputation is based on what other people think" (*Servant Leadership Models for Your Parish*, 23). As consciousness takes root, identity takes shape, and we are able to extend the kingdom of God to all we encounter with credibility. Credibility is power, and authentic power is service.

Consider how some of the following actions could give witness to your faith in Jesus Christ:

- Leading spontaneous prayer in which you express your trust and confidence in the Lord
- Sharing personal reflections in your newsletter, the parish bulletin, or the parish or program Web site, Facebook page, or Twitter account
- Inviting others to share their stories as well
- Acknowledging the contributions and achievements of others
- Sending notes, cards, and texts to thank people for sharing their gifts and to affirm them
- Paying attention to creature comforts and hospitality at faith-formation gatherings
- Stepping into the trenches and performing menial tasks without complaint

- Going out of your way to assist a catechist who is struggling
- Spending generous time with a family that is grieving or struggling
- Giving generous time to those who come to you for assistance
- Speaking respectfully about those with whom you disagree
- Acting with compassion toward those in need

The Signs and Symbols of Worship (*Leitourgia*)

The second aspect of the Catholic way of proceeding is the ease with which we allow the physical senses to be immersed in the mystery of faith. Catholics do this by learning a language of mystery that relies on signs and symbols. It is no surprise that people use signs and symbols, or visible items, to communicate abstract meanings. Earlier, I shared how I grew up learning the practices and traditions of Mexico. Two of these practices were singing the national anthem and saluting the flag. Singing and saluting the flag do not mean that one is worshiping the flag or one's country. Rather, they remind citizens of their civic duty and of a nation's highest ideals. In our personal relationships, we often rely on symbolic actions and gestures to express feelings and desires that words alone cannot capture. The same is true when it comes to expressing our feelings and desires for God: we use signs and symbols, that, for Catholics, are always present in liturgy.

In his book *Practice Makes Catholic*, Joe Paprocki identifies a number of practices that enable Catholics to "'put on' the eyes of Christ" (xi) and move from a learned faith to a lived faith. Many of these practices are examples of our sacramentality—our use of visible, tangible realities to express and encounter the invisible, intangible mystery of God. Examples include genuflecting, bowing, praying the sign of the cross, praying novenas, wearing a scapular, praying the rosary, blessing yourself with holy water, lighting candles, and so on. Because humankind has been created to know, love, and serve God, Catholics around the world express our deepest thoughts and desires about God with signs and symbols. While God is Spirit and therefore invisible and intangible, we human beings are embodied creatures who recognize that our expressions of realities such as love, acceptance, belonging, forgiveness, and commitment also need to be embodied. Therefore, Catholics use tangible, visible, and perceptible signs both to express and to encounter the mystery of God. In other words, "to be sacramental is to see the presence of God reflected in the physical world" (ibid., 6).

In a world that increasingly values only that which can be empirically validated, there can be a temptation to strip our Catholic faith of the more mystical aspects of our practice. As Bishop Robert Barron warns, however, we could easily fall into the trap of watering down our Catholic identity and values just to blend in with society. At the other extreme are those who nostalgically long for a return to all the "smells and bells" of the pre-Vatican II Church, as if those external trappings were the sole measure of Catholic identity.

As a catechetical leader, your task is to ensure that Catholic identity is truly balanced. Some of the ways you can do this include the following:

- Setting up a prayer space in your own office
- Creating a prayer center with signs and symbols (crucifix, Bible, candle, holy water, color of the liturgical season, etc.) for every faith-formation gathering
- Observing the seasons and feasts of the liturgical calendar (e.g., calling attention to the saint of the day)
- Inviting participants at faith-formation gatherings to engage in a ritual such as a procession to set up the prayer center
- Including silent reflection in faith-formation gatherings and prayer experiences

- Including the proclamation of Scripture and singing of Catholic hymns at faith-formation gatherings and prayer experiences
- Incorporating Catholic devotions such as a May Crowning, the Way of the Cross, and Adoration of the Blessed Sacrament into the faith-formation program
- Making sacred art a part of the decor of all faith-formation gathering spaces

Fiddo and Negrito

When I was growing up, I heard the following story told more than once by my pastor. In a secluded village in rural Mexico, there was an old priest who had been the pastor of a small church for more than fifteen years. People were happy with him, and every time he gave a homily, Fiddo and Negrito, his two cats, could be found right at his feet. When Father walked in procession on the Feast of Corpus Christi, Fiddo and Negrito processed right alongside him. If Father was praying the Rosary, Fiddo and Negrito were right there as well. For more than fifteen years, people in the village never questioned the presence of the cats but rather just went about their business and believed that this was part of the practice of the Church. Finally, the old pastor died, and a new priest was assigned. On his first Sunday at the church, the new pastor got up to deliver his homily. He had barely begun when an elderly woman raised her hand and asked why Fiddo and Negrito were not at his feet. The priest was puzzled by the question because he was not aware of the cats, so he simply continued with Mass. Later, someone told him about Fiddo and Negrito. During the week, he ran into the elderly woman as she participated in one of the parish ministries, and he asked her why she had brought up the two cats. She replied, "Father, sermons are boring. People are more interested in watching those two cats." My pastor used this story to teach that sometimes we Catholics focus more on the external and peripheral trappings of our faith than on how they are connected to the core of our faith. Our sacramental worship is crucial to our identity as Catholics but only when we embrace its full meaning. As a catechetical leader, one of your primary responsibilities is to catechize the community about the meaning of our sacramental signs, symbols, and rituals.

Service (*Diakonia*)

Catholic identity is also lived through the missionary activity of the Church. Because of the personal encounter disciples experience with the Lord, Catholics are compelled to transform and change the world we live in so as to ensure that all people experience God's abundant graces. History reveals that a number of institutions such as universities, hospitals, orphanages, and other charitable organizations were developed by the Catholic Church and are now vital to society. As I explored in the first chapter of this book, catechetical leaders are called to exercise servant leadership by serving the needs of others and by empowering people to follow Christ. Service is not something done out of pity for another, nor is it done so that we feel better about ourselves. Rather, charitable service is actually faith in action and giving witness to the Catholic faith in the public sphere. It is the act of bringing God's mercy to those who need it most. This service should be characterized by loving one another as Jesus has loved us (cf. John 13:34–35).

Last, serving in the name of Jesus Christ through the Church means being countercultural and embracing the way of the Cross. Although Catholics may have differences on certain issues that affect communities and society in general, we are all called to respect one another and to bring God's nearness to those who feel abandoned and vulnerable. As a catechetical leader, it is your responsibility to ensure that all those involved in faith formation are invited to participate in opportunities to be of service to others. It is crucial, likewise, to present these opportunities not as projects to be completed but as internships in a way of life.

As a catechetical leader, you can encourage *diakonia* (service) by doing the following:

- Incorporating service experiences (works of mercy) into every grade level of the faith-formation program as well as the RCIA (Rite of Christian Initiation for Adults) and adult faith-formation programs

- In your newsletter and on your Web site and Facebook page, highlighting children, teens, and adults engaged in service to others

- Promoting the concept of stewardship—the generous sharing of our time, talent, and treasure with the entire community

- Involving the parish community in charitable efforts with a catechetical angle, such as CRS Rice Bowl from Catholic Relief Services or Feed My Starving Children

- Inviting participation in efforts to promote social justice and respect for the dignity of human life from the moment of conception until natural death

Summary: The Spirit of the Lord Is upon Me

[Jesus said,] "The Spirit of the Lord is upon me,
because he has anointed me
to bring good news to the poor.
He has sent me to proclaim release to the captives
and recovery of sight to the blind,
to let the oppressed go free,
to proclaim the year of the Lord's favor" (Luke 4:18–19)

As catechetical leaders, we might be tempted to water down our Catholic identity in order to blend in with society—but we would do so at the risk of losing Christian values and personal integrity. Rather, as catechetical leaders, we are called to give credible (not triumphal) witness to the Catholic faith by living out the teachings of the Lord and by acting in ways that show compassion, mercy, and love of God and neighbor. Our Catholic way of proceeding, or modus operandi, is characterized by proclaiming the Word of God (*kerygma-martyria*), celebrating the sacraments (*leitourgia*), and living lives of service (*diakonia*).

For Reflection and Discussion

- What has been the greatest challenge of living your faith in your community?
- How do you give witness to your faith at home and in the public arena?

Growing as a Catechetical Leader

Living the Catholic faith is no easy road. The Church acknowledges that no one is perfect and that everyone makes mistakes along the way. Nevertheless, as Catholics, we are called to reconfigure ourselves to Christ every day and to see creation through the eyes of God. Doing so reinforces our Catholic identity and results in a coherent lifestyle based on the teachings of the Lord. What are personal areas you may need to work on to configure yourself to Christ?

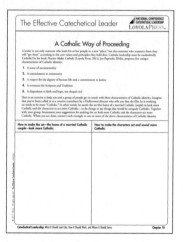

Go to www.loyolapress.com/ECL to access the worksheet.

Suggested Action

Praying with Scripture every day using the ancient method of *lectio divina* can be a starting point on your path to holiness. Try to spend fifteen minutes every day in this type of prayer. As author Gary Jansen explains in his book *The 15-Minute Prayer Solution*, "The more you enter into this direct communication with God, the easier it will become." If you already have this practice, try intentionally seeing things through the eyes of God. (Hint: The Beatitudes are a good lens.)

For Further Consideration

The Catholic Vision for Leading Like Jesus: Introducing S3 Leadership. Owen Phelps, PhD (Huntington, IN: Our Sunday Visitor, 2014).

Being Catholic Today: Catholic Identity in an Age of Challenge. Donald Cardinal Wuerl (Archdiocese of Washington, May 24, 2015).

Practice Makes Catholic: Moving from a Learned Faith to a Lived Faith. Joe Paprocki (Chicago: Loyola Press, 2011).

What Makes Us Catholic: Eight Gifts for Life. Thomas H. Groome (San Francisco: HarperOne, 2003).

The 15-Minute Prayer Solution: How One Percent of Your Day Can Transform Your Life. Gary Jansen (Chicago: Loyola Press, 2010).

About the Author

Adrián Alberto Herrera is an Associate Director for the Office of Evangelization and Catechesis in the Archdiocese of Galveston-Houston. He has served as consultant to the National Advisory Committee on Adult Religious Education, formerly known as NACARE. Author of *Oraciones y Reflexiones Dominicales para Católicos 2017*, he also developed materials for the USCCB Committee on Evangelization and Catechesis. He has been a catechist, youth minister, and Director of Religious Education.

The Effective Catechetical Leader Series

Whether you are starting out as a catechetical leader or have been serving as one for many years, **The Effective Catechetical Leader** series will help you use every aspect of this ministry to proclaim the Gospel and invite people to discipleship.

Called by Name
Preparing Yourself for the Vocation of Catechetical Leader

Catechetical Leadership
What It Should Look Like, How It Should Work, and Whom It Should Serve

Developing Disciples of Christ
Understanding the Critical Relationship between Catechesis and Evangelization

Cultivating Your Catechists
How to Recruit, Encourage, and Retain Successful Catechists

Excellence in Ministry
Best Practices for Successful Catechetical Leadership

All God's People
Effective Catechesis in a Diverse Church

Each book in **The Effective Catechetical Leader** series is available for $13.95, or the entire series is available for $65.00.

To Order:
Call **800.621.1008** or visit **loyolapress.com/ECL**

The ECL App

Everything You Need to Be an Effective Catechetical Leader

The ECL app puts wisdom and practical help at your fingertips. Drawn directly from the six books of **The Effective Catechetical Leader** series, ECL provides an opportunity for catechetical leaders to center themselves spiritually each day, focus on specific pastoral issues, and identify go-to strategies for meeting the challenges of serving as an effective catechetical leader.

Special Features:

- Over 40 unique guided reflections tailored to your individual pastoral ministry needs.
- On-the-go convenience and accessibility on your phone or tablet.
- Modern design, easy-to-use interface, and a source of calm amidst the busy schedule of a catechetical leader.

For more details and to download the app, visit
www.loyolapress.com/ECL